PENGUIN BOOKS — GREAT IDEAS

Sensation and Sex

Lucretius
c. 99–*c.* 55 BC

Lucretius

Sensation and Sex

TRANSLATED BY

R. E. LATHAM

PENGUIN BOOKS

Published by the Penguin Group
Penguin Books Ltd, 80 Strand, London WC2R ORL, England
Penguin Group (USA) Inc., 375 Hudson Street, New York, New York 10014, USA
Penguin Group (Canada), 10 Alcorn Avenue, Toronto, Ontario, Canada M4V 3B2
(a division of Pearson Penguin Canada Inc.)
Penguin Ireland, 25 St Stephen's Green, Dublin 2, Ireland
(a division of Penguin Books Ltd)
Penguin Group (Australia), 250 Camberwell Road,
Camberwell, Victoria 3124, Australia (a division of Pearson Australia Group Pty Ltd)
Penguin Books India Pvt Ltd, 11 Community Centre,
Panchsheel Park, New Delhi – 110 017, India
Penguin Group (NZ), cnr Airborne and Rosedale Roads, Albany,
Auckland 1310, New Zealand (a division of Pearson New Zealand Ltd)
Penguin Books (South Africa) (Pty) Ltd, 24 Sturdee Avenue,
Rosebank 2196, South Africa

Penguin Books Ltd, Registered Offices: 80 Strand, London WC2R ORL, England

www.penguin.com

On the Nature of the Universe first published in Penguin Classics 1951
This extract published in Penguin Books 2005
1

Translation copyright 1951 by R. E. Latham
All rights reserved

Taken from the Penguin Classics edition of *On the Nature of the Universe*,
translated and edited by R. E. Latham

Set by Rowland Phototypesetting Ltd, Bury St Edmunds, Suffolk
Printed in England by Clays Ltd, St Ives plc

Contents

Life and Mind

You, who out of black darkness were first to lift up a shining light, revealing the hidden blessings of life – you are my guide, O glory of the Grecian race. In your well-marked footprints now I plant my resolute steps. It is from love alone that I long to imitate you, not from emulous ambition. Shall the swallow contend in song with the swan, or the kid match its rickety legs in a race with the strong-limbed steed? You are my father, illustrious discoverer of truth, and give me a father's guidance. From your pages, as bees in flowery glades sip every blossom, so do I crop all your Golden Sayings – golden indeed, and for ever worthy of everlasting life.

As soon as your reasoning, sprung from that god-like mind, lifts up its voice to proclaim the nature of the universe, then the terrors of the mind take flight, the ramparts of the world roll apart, and I see the march of events throughout the whole of space. The majesty of the gods is revealed and those quiet habitations, never shaken by storms nor drenched by rain-clouds nor defaced by white drifts of snow which a harsh frost congeals. A cloudless ether roofs them, and laughs with radiance lavishly diffused. All their wants are supplied by nature, and nothing at any time cankers their peace of mind. But nowhere do I see the halls of Hell, though the earth is no barrier to my beholding all that passes underfoot in the space beneath. At this I am seized with a divine delight, and a shuddering awe, that by your power nature stands thus unveiled and made manifest in every part.

I have already shown what the component bodies of everything are like; how they vary in shape; how they fly spontaneously through space, impelled by a perpetual motion; and how from these all objects can be created. The next step now is evidently to elucidate in my verses the nature of mind and of life. In so doing I shall drive out neck and crop that fear of Hell which blasts the life of man from its very foundations, sullying everything with the blackness of death and leaving no pleasure pure and unalloyed. I know that men often speak of sickness or of shameful life as more to be dreaded than the terrors of Hell; they profess to know that the mind consists of blood, or maybe wind, if that is how the whim takes them, and to stand in no need whatever of our reasoning. But all this talk is based more on a desire to show off than on actual proof, as you may infer from their conduct. These same men, though they may be exiled from home, banished far from the sight of their fellows, soiled with some filthy crime, a prey to every torment, still cling to life. Wherever they come in their tribulation, they make propitiatory sacrifices, slaughter black cattle and dispatch offerings to the Departed Spirits. The heavier their afflictions, the more devoutly they turn their minds to superstition. Look at a man in the midst of doubt and danger, and you will learn in his hour of adversity what he really is. It is then that true utterances are wrung from the recesses of his breast. The mask is torn off; the reality remains.

Consider too the greed and blind lust of power that drive unhappy men to overstep the bounds of right and may even turn them into accomplices or instruments of crime, struggling night and day with unstinted effort to scale the pinnacles of wealth. These running sores of life are fed in no small measure by the fear of death. For abject ignominy and irksome poverty seem far indeed from the joy and assurance of life, and in effect loitering already at the gateway of death. From such a fate men revolt in groundless terror and long to escape far, far away. So in their greed of gain they amass a fortune out of civil bloodshed: piling wealth on wealth, they heap carnage on carnage. With heartless glee they welcome a brother's tragic death. They hate and fear the hospitable board of their own kin. Often, in the same spirit and influenced by the same fear, they are consumed with envy at the sight of another's success: he walks in a blaze of glory, looked up to by all, while they curse the dingy squalor in which their own lives are bogged. Some sacrifice life itself for the sake of statues and a title. Often from fear of death mortals are gripped by such a hate of living and looking on the light that with anguished hearts they do themselves to death. They forget that this very fear is the fountainhead of their troubles; this it is that harasses conscience, snaps the bonds of friendship and hurls down virtue from the heights. Many a time before now men have betrayed their country and their beloved parents in an effort to escape the halls of Hell.

As children in blank darkness tremble and start at

everything, so we in broad daylight are oppressed at times by fears as baseless as those horrors which children imagine coming upon them in the dark. This dread and darkness of the mind cannot be dispelled by the sunbeams, the shining shafts of day, but only by an understanding of the outward form and inner workings of nature.

First, I maintain that *the mind*, which we often call the intellect, the seat of the guidance and control of life, *is part of a man*, no less than hand or foot or eyes are parts of a whole living creature. There are some who argue that the sentience of the mind is not lodged in any particular part, but is a vital condition of the body, what the Greeks call a *harmony*, which makes us live as sentient beings without having any locally determined mind. Just as good health may be said to belong to the healthy body without being any specific part of it, so they do not station the sentience of the mind in any specific part. In this they seem to me very wide of the mark. Often enough the visible body is obviously ill, while in some other unseen part we are enjoying ourselves. No less often the reverse happens: one who is sick at heart enjoys bodily well-being. This is no different from the experience of an invalid whose foot is hurting while his head is in no pain.

Or consider what happens when we have surrendered our limbs to soothing slumber and our body, replete and relaxed, lies insensible. At that very time there is something else in us that is awake to all sorts of stimuli

– something that gives free admittance to all the motions of joy and to heart-burnings void of substance.

Next, you must understand that *there is also a vital spirit in our limbs* and the body does not derive its sentience from harmony. In the first place, life often lingers in our limbs after a large part of the body has been cut off. On the other hand, when a few particles of heat have dispersed and some air has been let out through the mouth, life forsakes the veins forthwith and abandons the bones. Hence you may infer that all the elements do not hold equal portions of vitality or sustain it equally, but it is chiefly thanks to the atoms of wind and heat that life lingers in the limbs. There is therefore in the body itself a vital breath and heat which forsakes our limbs at death.

Now that we have discovered the nature of the mind and of the vital spirit as a part of the man, drop this name harmony which was passed down to the musicians from the heights of Helicon – or else perhaps they fetched it themselves from some other source and applied it to the matter of their art, which had then no name of its own. Whatever it be, let them keep it. And give your attention now to the rest of my discourse.

Next, I maintain that *mind and spirit are interconnected* and compose between them a single substance. But what I may call the head and the dominant force in the whole body is that guiding principle which we term mind or intellect. This is firmly lodged in the mid-region of the breast. Here is the place where fear and alarm pulsate. Here is felt the caressing touch of joy. Here, then, is the seat of intellect and mind. The rest of the vital spirit, diffused throughout the body, obeys the mind and moves under its direction and impulse. The mind by itself experiences thought and joy of its own at a time when nothing moves either the body or the spirit.

When our head or eye suffers from an attack of pain, our whole body does not share in its aching. Just so the mind sometimes suffers by itself or jumps for joy when the rest of the spirit, diffused through every limb and member, is not stirred by any new impulse. But, when the mind is upset by some more overwhelming fear, we see all the spirit in every limb upset in sympathy. Sweat and pallor break out all over the body. Speech grows inarticulate; the voice fails; the eyes swim; the ears buzz; the limbs totter. Often we see men actually drop down because of the terror that has gripped their minds. Hence you may readily infer a connexion between the mind and the spirit which, when shaken by the impact of the mind, immediately jostles and propels the body.

The same reasoning proves that *mind and spirit are both composed of matter*. We see them propelling the limbs, rousing the body from sleep, changing the expression of the face and guiding and steering the whole man – activities that all clearly involve touch, as touch in turn involves matter. How then can we deny their material nature? You see the mind sharing in the body's experiences and sympathizing with it. When the nerve-racking impact of a spear gashes bones and sinews, even if it does not penetrate to the seat of life, there ensues faintness and a tempting inclination earthwards and on the ground a turmoil in the mind and an intermittent faltering impulse to stand up again. The substance of the mind must therefore be material, since it is affected by the impact of material weapons.

My next task will be to demonstrate to you what sort of matter it is of which this mind is composed and how it was formed. First, I affirm that *it is of very fine texture and composed of exceptionally minute particles*. If you will mark my words, you will be able to infer this from the following facts. It is evident that nothing happens as quickly as the mind represents and sketches the happening to itself. Therefore the mind sets itself in motion more swiftly than any of those things whose substance is visible to our eyes. But what is so mobile must consist of exceptionally minute and spherical atoms, so that it can be set going by a slight push. The reason why water is set going and flowing by such a slight push is of course the smallness of its atoms and their readiness to roll. The stickier consistency of honey – its relatively sluggish flow and dilatory progress – is due to the closer coherence of the component matter, consisting, as it obviously does, of particles not so smooth or so fine or so round. A high pile of poppy seed can be disturbed by a light puff of breeze, so that it trickles down from the top, whereas a heap of stones or corn ears remains immovable. In proportion as objects are smaller and smoother, so much the more do they enjoy mobility; the greater their weight and roughness, the more firmly are they anchored. Since, therefore, the substance of the mind has been found to be extraordinarily mobile, it must consist of particles exceptionally small and smooth and round. This discovery, my dear fellow, will prove a timely aid to you in many problems.

Here is a further indication how flimsy is the texture of the vital spirit and in how small a space it could be contained if it could be massed together. At the instant when a man is mastered by the care-free calm of death and forsaken by mind and spirit, you cannot tell either by sight or by weight that any part of the whole has been filched away from his body. Death leaves everything there, except vital sentience and warmth. Therefore the vital spirit as a whole must consist of very tiny atoms, linked together throughout veins, flesh and sinews – atoms so small that, when all the spirit has escaped from the whole body, the outermost contour of the limbs appears intact and there is no loss of weight. The same thing happens when the bouquet has evaporated from the juice of Bacchus, or the sweet perfume of an ointment has escaped into the air, or some substance has lost its savour. The substance itself is not visibly diminished by the loss, and its weight is not lessened, obviously because savour and scent are caused by many minute atoms distributed throughout the mass. On every ground, therefore, it may be inferred that mind and spirit are composed of exceptionally diminutive atoms, since their departure is not accompanied by any loss of weight.

*

It must not be supposed that the stuff of mind or spirit is a single element. The body at death is abandoned by a sort of rarefied wind mixed with warmth, while the warmth carries with it also air. Indeed, heat never occurs without an intermixture of air: because it is naturally sparse, it must have many atoms of air moving in its interstices.

The composition of mind is thus found to be *at least three-fold*. But all these three components together are not enough to create sentience, since the mind does not admit that any of these can create the sensory motions that originate the meditations revolved in the mind. *We must* accordingly *add to these a fourth component*, which is quite nameless. Than this there is nothing more mobile or more tenuous – nothing whose component atoms are smaller or smoother. This it is that first sets the sensory motions coursing through the limbs. Owing to the minuteness of its atoms, it is first to be stirred. Then the motions are caught up by warmth and the unseen energy of wind, then by air. Then everything is roused to movement: the blood is quickened; the impulse spread throughout the flesh; last of all, bones and marrow are thrilled with pleasure or the opposite excitement. To this extremity pain cannot lightly penetrate, or the pangs of anguish win through. If they do, then everything is so confounded that no room is left for life, and the components of the vital spirit escape through all the pores of the body. But usually a stop is put to these movements as near as may be at the surface of the body. Thanks to this stoppage we contrive to cling on to life.

*

At this point I should like to demonstrate *how these components are intermixed* and from what mode of combination they derive their powers. Reluctantly I am thwarted in my purpose by the poverty of our native tongue. But, so far as I can touch upon the surface of this topic, I will tackle it.

The atoms rush in and out among one another on atomic trajectories, so that no one of them can be segregated nor its distinctive power isolated by intervening space. They co-exist like the many properties of a single body. In the flesh of any living thing there are regularly scent and colour and taste; and yet from all these there is formed only one corporeal bulk. Just so, warmth and air and the unseen energy of wind create in combination a single substance, together with that mobile force which imparts to them from itself the initial impetus from which the sensory motion takes its rise throughout the flesh. This basic substance lurks at our very core. There is nothing in our bodies more fundamental than this, the most vital element of their whole vital spirit. Just as in our limbs and body as a whole mind and spirit with their interconnected powers are latent, because their component atoms are small and sparse, so this nameless element composed of minute atoms is latent in the vital spirit and is in turn its vital element and controls the whole body.

In the same way, wind and air and warmth commingled through the limbs must interact, one being relatively latent, another prominent. In appearance a single stuff is formed by them all: warmth and wind and air do not display their powers separately so as to blot out sentience and dissolve it by their disunion. First, there is at the mind's disposal that element of heat which it brings into play when it boils with rage and passion blazes more fiercely from the eyes. There is likewise no lack of that chill wind, associated with fear, which sets the limbs atremble and impels them to flight. There is lastly that calm and steady air which prevails in a tranquil breast and unruffled mien.

In those creatures whose passionate hearts and choleric dispositions easily boil up in anger, there is a surplus of the hot element. An outstanding example is the truculent temper of lions, who often roar till they burst their chests with bellowing and cannot keep the torrents of their rage pent within. But the cold hearts of deer are of a windier blend: they are quicker to set chill breezes blowing through the flesh, provoking a shuddering movement in the limbs. Cattle, again, have in their vital composition a bigger portion of calm air. They are never too hotly fired by a touch of that smoky torch of anger which clouds the mind with its black and blinding shadow. They are never transfixed and benumbed by the icy shaft of fear. Their nature is a mean between the timidity of the deer and the lion's ferocity.

So it is with men. Though education may apply a similar polish to various individuals, it still leaves fundamental traces of their several temperaments. It must not be supposed that innate vices can be completely eradicated: one man will still incline more readily to outbursts of rage; another will give way a little sooner to fear; a third will accept some contingencies too impassively. And in a host of other ways men must differ one from another in temperament and so also in the resultant behaviour. To unfold here the secret causes of these differences is beyond my power. I cannot even find names for the multiplicity of atomic shapes that give rise to this variety of types. But I am clear that there is one relevant fact I can affirm: the lingering traces of inborn temperament that cannot be eliminated by philosophy are so slight that there is nothing to prevent men from leading a life worthy of the gods.

This *vital spirit*, then, *is present in the whole body*. It is the body's guardian and preserver. For the two are interlocked by common roots and cannot be torn apart without manifest disaster. As easily could the scent be torn out of lumps of incense without destroying their nature as mind and spirit could be abstracted from the whole body without total dissolution. So from their earliest origin the two are charged with a communal life by the intertangled atoms that compose them. It is clear that neither body nor mind by itself without the other's aid possesses the power of sensation: it is by the interacting motions of the two combined that the flame of sentience is kindled in our flesh.

Again, body by itself never experiences birth or growth, and we see that it does not persist after death. Water, we know, often gives up the heat imparted to it without being disrupted in the process, and survives intact. Not so can the derelict limbs outlast the departure of the vital spirit: they are utterly demolished by internal decomposition and decay. So from the very beginning, even when they are at rest in the mother's womb, body and spirit in mutual contact acquire the motions that generate life. They cannot be wrenched apart without hurt and havoc. So you may see, since their very existence depends upon conjunction, that their nature must likewise be conjoint.

If anyone still denies that the body is sentient, and believes it is the spirit interfused throughout the body that assumes this motion which we term sensation, he is fighting against manifest facts. Who can explain what bodily sensation really is, if it is not such as it is palpably presented to us by experience? Admittedly, when the spirit is banished, the body is quite insensible. That is because what it loses was never one of its permanent properties, but one of many attributes which it loses at death.

Again, it is awkward to maintain that the eyes can see nothing, but the mind peeps out through them as though through open doors. The sense of sight itself leads us the other way, dragging and tugging us right to the eyeballs. Often, for instance, we cannot see bright objects, because our eyes are dazzled by light. This is an experience unknown to doors: the doorways through which we gaze suffer no distress by being flung open. Besides, if our eyes are equivalent to doors, then when the eyes are removed the mind obviously ought to see things better now that the doors are away, doorposts and all.

Another error to be avoided, and one that is sanctioned by the revered authority of the great Democritus, is the belief that the limbs are knit together by atoms of body and mind arranged alternately, first one and then the other. In fact, *the atoms of spirit are not only much less in magnitude than those composing our body and flesh; they are also correspondingly inferior in number* and scattered but sparsely through our limbs. Observe what are the smaller objects whose impact serves to excite sensory motions in our bodies: these will give you the measure of the gaps between the atoms of spirit. Sometimes we are unaware that dust is sticking to our bodies or a cloud of chalk has settled on our limbs; we do not feel the night mist, or the slight threads of gossamer in our path that enmesh us as we walk, or the fall of a flimsy cobweb on our heads, or plumes of birds or flying thistle-down, which from their very lightness do not lightly descend. We do not mark the path of every creeping thing that crawls across our body or every separate footfall planted by a gnat or midge. So quite a considerable commotion must be made in our bodies before the atomic disturbance is felt by the atoms of spirit interspersed through our limbs and before these can knock together across the intervening gaps and clash and combine and again bounce apart.

Note also that *it is mind, far more than spirit, that keeps life under lock and key* – mind that has the greater mastery over life. Without mind and intellect no scrap of vital spirit can linger one instant in our limbs. Spirit follows smoothly in the wake of mind and scatters into the air, leaving the limbs cold with the chill of death. While mind remains, life remains. One whose limbs are all lopped from the mangled trunk, despite the loss of vital spirit released from the limbs, yet lives and inhales the life-giving gusts of air. Though robbed, if not of all, at least of a large proportion of his spirit, he lingers still in life and clings fast to it. Just so, though the eye is lacerated all round, so long as the pupil remains intact, the faculty of vision remains alive, provided always that you do not hack away the whole encircling orb and leave the eyeball detached and isolated; for that cannot be done without total destruction. But tamper with that tiny bit in the middle of the eye, and out goes the light there and then and darkness falls, although the shining orb is otherwise unscathed. It is on just such terms that spirit and mind are everlastingly linked together.

My next point is this: you must understand that the *minds of living things and the light fabric of their spirits are neither birthless nor deathless*. To this end I have long been mustering and inventing verses with a labour that is also a joy. Now I will try to set them out in a style worthy of your career.

Please note that both objects are to be embraced under one name. When, for instance, I proceed to demonstrate that 'spirit' is mortal, you must understand that this applies equally to 'mind', since the two are so conjoined as to constitute a single substance.

First of all, then, I have shown that spirit is flimsy stuff composed of tiny particles. Its atoms are obviously far smaller than those of swift-flowing water or mist or smoke, since it far outstrips them in mobility and is moved by a far slighter impetus. Indeed, it is actually moved by images of smoke and mist. So, for instance, when we are sunk in sleep, we may see altars sending up clouds of steam and giving off smoke; and we cannot doubt that we are here dealing with images. Now, we see that water flows out in all directions from a broken vessel and the moisture is dissipated, and mist and smoke vanish into thin air. Be assured, therefore, that spirit is similarly dispelled and vanishes far more speedily and is sooner dissolved into its component atoms once it has been let loose from the human frame. When the body, which served as a vessel for it, is by some means broken and attenuated by loss of blood from the veins, so as to be no longer able to contain it, how can you suppose that it can be contained by any kind of air, which must be far more tenuous than our bodily frame?

Again, we are conscious that mind and body are born together, grow up together and together decay. With the weak and delicate frame of wavering childhood goes a like infirmity of judgement. The robust vigour of ripening years is accompanied by a steadier resolve and a maturer strength of mind. Later, when the the body is palsied by the potent forces of age and the limbs begin to droop with blunted vigour, the understanding limps, the tongue falters and the mind totters: everything weakens and gives way at the same time. It is thus natural that the vital spirit should all evaporate like smoke, soaring into the gusty air, since we have seen that it shares the body's birth and growth and wearies with the weariness of age.

Furthermore, as the body suffers the horrors of disease and the pangs of pain, so we see the mind stabbed with anguish, grief and fear. What more natural than that it should likewise have a share in death? Often enough in the body's illness the mind wanders. It raves and babbles distractedly. At times it drifts on a tide of drowsiness, with drooping eyelids and nodding head, into a deep and endless sleep, from which it cannot hear the voices or recognize the faces of those who stand around with streaming eyes and tear-stained cheeks, striving to recall it to life. Since the mind is thus invaded by the contagion of disease, you must acknowledge that it is destructible. For pain and sickness are the artificers of death, as we have been taught by the fate of many men before us.

Again, when the pervasive power of wine has entered into a man and its glow is dispersed through his veins, his limbs are overcome by heaviness; his legs stagger and stumble; his speech is slurred, his mind besotted; his eyes swim; there is a crescendo of shouts, hiccups, oaths; and all the other symptoms follow in due order. Why should this be, if not because the wanton wildness of the wine has power to dislodge the vital spirit within the body? And, when things can be dislodged and arrested, this is an indication that the inroad of a slightly more potent force would make an end of them and rob them of a future.

Or it may happen that a man is seized with a sudden spasm of epilepsy before our eyes. He falls as though struck by lightning and foams at the mouth. He groans and trembles in every joint. He raves. He contracts his muscles. He writhes. He gasps convulsively. He tires his limbs with tossing. The cause of the foaming is that the force of the disease, dispersed through the limbs, dislodges the vital spirit and lashes it to spray, as the wild wind's fury froths the salt sea waves. The groans are wrung from him because his limbs are racked with pain and in general because atoms of vocal sound are expelled and whirled out in a lump through the mouth – their customary outlet, where the way is already paved for them. The raving occurs because mind and spirit are dislodged and, as I have explained, split up and scattered this way and that by the same toxin. Then, when the cause of the disease has passed its climax and the morbid secretion of the distempered body ebbs back to its secret abode, then the man rises, swaying unsteadily at first, and returns bit by bit to all his senses and recovers his vital spirit. When mind and spirit in the body itself are a prey to such violent maladies and suffer such distressing dispersal, how can you believe them capable of surviving apart from the body in the open air with the wild winds for company?

Conversely, we see that the mind, like a sick body, can be healed and directed by medicine. This too is a presage that its life is mortal. When you embark on an attempt to alter the mind or to direct any other natural object, it is fair to suppose that you are adding certain parts or transposing them or subtracting some trifle at any rate from their sum. But an immortal object will not let its parts be rearranged or added to, or the least bit drop off. For, if ever anything is so transformed as to overstep its own limits, this means the immediate death of what was before. By this susceptibility both to sickness (as I have shown) and to medicine, the mind displays the marks of mortality. So false reasoning is plainly confronted by true fact. Every loophole is barred to its exponent, and by the two horns of a dilemma he is convicted of falsehood.

Again, we often see a man pass away little by little, and lose his vital sensibility limb by limb: first the toes and toenails lose their colour; then the feet and legs die; after that the imprint of icy death steals by slow degrees through the other members. Since the vital spirit is thus dispersed and does not come out all at once in its entirety, it must be regarded as mortal. You may be tempted to suppose that it can shrink into itself through the body and draw its parts together and so withdraw sensibility from every limb. But, if that were so, the place in which such a mass of spirit was concentrated ought to display an exceptional degree of sensibility. Since there is no such place, it evidently leaks out in driblets, as I said before – in other words, it perishes. Let us, however, concede this false hypothesis and suppose that the spirit concentrates within the body of those who leave the light of day through a creeping palsy. You must still acknowledge that spirit is mortal. It makes no odds whether it is scattered to the winds and disintegrated, or concentrated and deadened. In either case, the victim as a whole is more and more drained of sensibility in every part, and in every part less and less of life remains.

The mind, again, is a part of a man and stays fixed in a particular spot, no less than the ears and eyes and other senses by which life is guided. Now, our hand or eye or nostrils in isolation from us cannot experience sensation or even exist; in a very short time they rot away. So mind cannot exist apart from body and from the man himself who is, as it were, a vessel for it – or if you choose you may picture it as something still more intimately linked, since body clings to mind by close ties.

Again, mind and body as a living force derive their vigour and vitality from their conjunction. Without body, the mind alone cannot perform the vital motions. Bereft of vital spirit, the body cannot persist and exercise its senses. As the eye uprooted and separated from the body cannot see, so we perceive that spirit and mind by themselves are powerless. It is only because their atoms are held in by the whole body, intermingled through veins and flesh, sinews and bones, and are not free to bounce far apart, that they are kept together so as to perform the motions that generate sentience. After death, when they are expelled out of the body into the gusty air, they cannot perform the sensory motions because they are no longer held together in the same way. The air indeed will itself be a body, and an animate one at that, if it allows the vital spirit to hang together and keep up these motions which it used to go through before in the sinews and the body itself. Here then is proof upon proof. You must perforce admit that, when the whole bodily envelope crumbles after the expulsion of the vital breath, the senses of the mind and the spirit likewise disintegrate, since body and mind are effects of the same cause.

Again, the body cannot suffer the withdrawal of the vital spirit without rotting away in a foul stench. How can you doubt, then, but that the spirit diffused in the depths of the body has come to the surface and evaporated like smoke? That explains why the body is transformed and collapses so utterly into decay: its inmost foundations are sapped by the effusion of the spirit through the limbs and through all the body's winding channels and chinks. So there are many indications that the vital spirit seeps out through the limbs in driblets and is already split up within the body before it slips out and glides into the gusty air.

No one on the point of death seems to feel his spirit retiring intact right out of his body or rising first to his gullet and up through his throat. On the contrary, he feels that it is failing in a particular region which it occupies, just as he is conscious that his other senses are being extinguished each in its own sphere. If our mind were indeed immortal, it would not complain of extinction in the hour of death, but would feel rather that it was escaping from confinement and sloughing off its garment like a snake.

Even while the vital spirit yet lingers within the boundaries of life, it often seems, when something has violently upset it, as though it were struggling to escape and be wholly released from the body – as though the features were relaxing into their ultimate immobility and every limb were ready to hang limp upon the bloodless trunk. It is at such times that we say 'the mind has had a shock' or 'the spirit has fled'. The fear of death is already upon us, and everyone is straining to hold fast the last link with life. Then the mind and all the vital spirit are churned up and both these, together with the body, are on the point of collapse, so that a slightly intensified force might shatter them. How can you doubt, then, that the fragile spirit once stripped of its envelope and thrust out of the body into the open would be powerless not only to survive throughout eternity but even to persist for a single instant?

Again, why is mind or thought never born in head or feet or hands? Why does it cling fast in every man to one spot or a specified region? It can only be that a specific place is assigned to each thing where it can be born and survive. So every creature is created with a great diversity of members, whose mutual position is never reversed. One thing duly follows another: flame is not born in a flood, nor frost begotten in fire.

Moreover, if the spirit is by nature immortal and can remain sentient when divorced from our body, we must credit it, I presume, with the possession of five senses. In no other way can we picture to ourselves departed spirits wandering through the Infernal Regions. So it is that painters and bygone generations of writers have portrayed spirits in possession of their senses. But eyes or nostrils or hand or tongue or ears cannot be attached to a disembodied spirit. Such a spirit cannot therefore be sentient or so much as exist.

We feel that vital sentience resides in the body as a whole and we see that the whole body is animate. Suppose, then, that it is suddenly sliced through the middle by some swiftly delivered slash, so as to fall into two quite separate parts. Without doubt the vital spirit will also be severed and split in two along with the body. But what is cleft and falls apart obviously resigns all pretensions that its nature is immortal. They say that in the heat and indiscriminate carnage of battle limbs are often lopped off by scythe-armed chariots so suddenly that the fallen member hewn from the body is seen to writhe on the ground. Yet the mind and consciousness of the man cannot yet feel the pain: so abrupt is the hurt, and so intent the mind upon the business of battle. With what is left of his body he presses on with battle and bloodshed unaware, it may be, that his left arm together with its shield has been lost, whirled away among the chargers by the chariot wheels with their predatory blades. Another does not notice that his right arm has gone, while he scrambles and struggles. Another, who has lost a leg, does his best to stand up, while on the ground at his side the dying foot twitches its toes. A head hewn from the still warm and living trunk retains on the ground its lively features and open eyes till it has yielded up the last shred of spirit. Or take for example a snake with flickering tongue, menacing tail and protracted body. Should you choose to hack it in many pieces with a blade, you will see, while the wound is fresh, every severed portion separately squirming and spattering the ground with gore, and the foremost part twisting back with its mouth to bite itself in the fierce agony of the wound. Shall we say that in each of these parts there is an entire spirit? But on that hypothesis it would follow that one animate creature had in its body many spirits. Actually, a spirit that was one has been split up along with the body. So both alike must be reckoned mortal, since both alike are split into many parts.

Next, if the spirit is by nature immortal and is slipped into the body at birth, why do we retain no memory of an earlier existence, no impress of antecedent events? If the mind's operation is so greatly changed that all record of former actions has been expunged, it is no long journey, in my judgement, from this experience to annihilation. So you must admit that the pre-existent spirit has died and the one that is now is a new creation.

Let us suppose, for argument's sake, that the vital force of mind is introduced into us when the body is already fully formed, at the moment when we are born and step across the threshold of life. This theory does not square with the observed fact that the mind grows with the bodily frame and in the very blood. It would imply that the mind lived in solitary confinement, alone in its cell, and yet at the same time the whole body was shot through with sentience. Here then is proof upon proof that spirits are not to be regarded as birthless, nor yet as exempt from the law of death. If they were slipped into our bodies from outside, it cannot be supposed that the two would be so closely interlocked as they are shown to be by the clearest evidence. For spirit so interpenetrates veins, flesh, sinews, bones, that our very teeth share in sensation – witness toothache and the shock of contact with icy water or a jagged stone buried in a loaf. Being thus interwoven, it does not seem possible that it should escape intact and extricate itself undamaged from every sinew, bone and joint. Or, if you suppose that, after being slipped in from outside, the spirit oozes through our limbs, then it is all the more bound to perish with the body through which it is thus interfused. To ooze through something is to be dissolved in it and therefore to perish. We know that food, when it is rationed out amongst our limbs and members by diffusion through all the channels of the body, is destroyed and takes on a different nature. Just so, on the assumption that spirit and mind enter into the newly formed body as complete entities, they must be dissolved in oozing through it: our limbs must be interpenetrated through every channel by the particles composing this mind which lords it now in our body – this new mind born of the old one that must have perished in its diffusion through our limbs. It is thus evident that the human spirit is neither independent of a birthday nor immune from a latter end.

The further question arises whether or not any atoms of vital spirit are left in a lifeless body. If some are left and lodge there, we are not justified in regarding the spirit as immortal, since it has come away mutilated by the loss of some of its parts. If, on the other hand, it withdraws with its members intact, so that no scrap of it remains in the body, how is it that corpses, when their flesh begins to rot, exude maggots? What is the source of that boneless and bloodless horde of animate things that swarms through the swollen limbs? You may argue that spirits can slip into the maggots from outside and settle individually in their bodies. I will not ask why in that case many thousands of spirits should forgather in the place from which one has withdrawn. But there is another question that calls for a decisive answer. Do these supposed spirits each hunt out atoms of maggots and manufacture dwelling-places for themselves? Or do they slip into ready-made bodies? No adequate reason can be given why they should undertake the labour of manufacture. In their bodiless state they presumably flit about untroubled by sickness, cold or hunger. For the body is far more subject to these afflictions, and

communion with it is the source of many of the mind's
troubles. But suppose they had the best of reasons for
making a body to which they could subject themselves:
there is no discernible way in which they could set about
it. So much for the suggestion that spirits make bodies
and limbs for themselves. We may equally rule out the
alternative theory that they slip into ready-made bodies.
For this would not account for the intimate communion
between body and spirit and their sensory interaction.

Again, why is grim ferocity an attribute of the lions'
surly breed, as craftiness of foxes? Why are deer endowed
by their parents with timidity and their limbs impelled
to flight by hereditary tremors? Why are all other traits
of this sort implanted in physique and character from
birth? It can only be because the mind always shares in
the specific growth of the body according to its seed and
breed. If it were immortal and passed from body to body,
there would be living things of jumbled characters. Often
the hound of Hyrcanian breed would turn tail before the
onset of the antlered stag. The hawk would flee trembling through the gusty air at the coming of the dove.
Man would be witless, and brute beasts rational. It is an
untenable theory that an immortal spirit is modified by
a change of body. For whatever changes is disintegrated
and therefore destroyed. The component parts of spirits
are in any case transposed and reshuffled. So the spirits
as a whole might just as well be diffused through the
limbs and eventually destroyed with the body. If, on
the other hand, it is maintained that the spirits of men
enter none but human bodies, then I would ask why a
wise one should become foolish – why a child is never

rational, nor a mare's foal as accomplished as a sturdy steed. The one loophole left is the assumption that in a frail body the mind too grows frail. But in that case you must admit that the spirit is mortal, since in its adaptation to the bodily frame it loses so utterly its previous vitality and sensibility. How can the mind wax stronger in unison with each particular body till it attains with it the coveted season of full bloom, unless the two are coheirs of a single birth? Why, when the limbs are wasted with age, should the mind wish to slip out and away? Is it afraid to stay locked up in a mouldering body? Afraid that its lodging may collapse from the wear and tear of age? Surely an immortal being need fear no danger.

Again, it is surely ludicrous to suppose that spirits are standing by at the mating and birth of animals – a numberless number of immortals on the look-out for mortal frames, jostling and squabbling to get in first and establish themselves most firmly. Or is there perhaps an established compact that first come shall be first served, without any trial of strength between spirit and spirit?

A tree cannot exist high in air, or clouds in the depths of the sea, as fish cannot live in the fields, or blood flow in wood or sap in stones. There is a determined and allotted place for the growth and presence of everything. So mind cannot arise alone without body or apart from sinews and blood. If it could do this, then surely it could much more readily function in head or shoulders or the tips of the heels and be born in any other part, so long as it was held in the same container, that is to say in the same man. Since, however, even in the human body we see a determined and allotted place set aside for the growth and presence of spirit and mind, we have even stronger grounds for denying that they could survive or come to birth outside the body altogether. You must admit, therefore, that when the body has perished there is an end also of the spirit diffused through it. It is surely crazy to couple a mortal object with an eternal and suppose that they can work in harmony and mutually interact. What can be imagined more incongruous, what more repugnant and discordant, than that a mortal object and one that is immortal and everlasting should unite to form a compound and jointly weather the storms that rage about them?

Again, there can be only three kinds of everlasting objects. The first, owing to the absolute solidity of their substance, can repel blows and let nothing penetrate them so as to unknit their close texture from within. Such are the atoms of matter, whose nature I have already demonstrated. The second kind can last for ever because it is immune from blows. Such is empty space, which remains untouched and unaffected by any impact. Last is that which has no available place surrounding it into which its matter can disperse and disintegrate. It is for this reason that the sum total of the universe is everlasting, having no space outside it into which the matter can escape and no matter that can enter and disintegrate it by the force of impact.

Equally vain is the suggestion that the spirit is immortal because it is shielded by life-preserving powers; or because it is unassailed by forces hostile to its survival; or because such forces, if they threaten, are somehow arrested before we are conscious of the threat. Apart from the spirit's participation in the ailments of the body, it has maladies enough of its own. The prospect of the future torments it with fear and wearies it with worry, and past misdeeds leave the sting of remorse. Lastly, it may fall a prey to the mind's own specific afflictions, madness and amnesia, and plunge into the black waters of oblivion.

From all this it follows that *death is nothing to us* and no concern of ours, since our tenure of the mind is mortal. In days of old, we felt no disquiet when the hosts of Carthage poured in to battle on every side – when the whole earth, dizzied by the convulsive shock of war, reeled sickeningly under the high ethereal vault, and between realm and realm the empire of mankind by land and sea trembled in the balance. So, when we shall be no more – when the union of body and spirit that engenders us has been disrupted – to us, who shall then be nothing, nothing by any hazard will happen any more at all. Nothing will have power to stir our senses, not though earth be fused with sea and sea with sky.

If any feeling remains in mind or spirit after it has been torn from our body, that is nothing to us, who are brought into being by the wedlock of body and spirit, conjoined and coalesced. Or even if the matter that composes us should be reassembled by time after our death and brought back into its present state – if the light of life were given to us anew – even that contingency would still be no concern of ours once the chain of our identity had been snapped. We who are now are not concerned with ourselves in any previous existence: the sufferings of those selves do not touch us. When you look at the immeasurable extent of time gone by and the multiform movements of matter, you will readily credit that these same atoms that compose us now must many a time before have entered into the self-same combinations as now. But our mind cannot recall this to remembrance. For between then and now is interposed a breach in life, and all the atomic motions have been wandering far astray from sentience.

If the future holds travail and anguish in store, the self must be in existence, when that time comes, in order to experience it. But from this fate we are redeemed by death, which denies existence to the self that might have suffered these tribulations. Rest assured, therefore, that we have nothing to fear in death. One who no longer is cannot suffer, or differ in any way from one who has never been born, when once this mortal life has been usurped by death the immortal.

When you find a man treating it as a grievance that after death he will either moulder in the grave or fall a prey to flames or to the jaws of predatory beasts, be sure that his utterance does not ring true. Subconsciously his heart is stabbed by a secret dread, however loudly the man himself may disavow the belief that after death he will still experience sensation. I am convinced that he does not grant the admission he professes, nor the grounds of it; he does not oust and pluck himself root and branch out of life, but all unwittingly makes something of himself linger on. When a living man confronts the thought that after death his body will be mauled by birds and beasts of prey, he is filled with self-pity. He does not banish himself from the scene nor distinguish sharply enough between himself and that abandoned carcass. He visualizes that object as himself and infects it with his own feelings as an onlooker. That is why he is aggrieved at having been created mortal. He does not see that in real death there will be no other self alive to mourn his own decease – no other self standing by to flinch at the agony he suffers lying there being mangled, or indeed being cremated. For if it is really a bad thing after death to be mauled and crunched by ravening jaws, I cannot see why it should not be disagreeable to roast in the scorching flames of a funeral pyre, or to lie embalmed in honey, stifled and stiff with cold, on the surface of a chilly slab, or to be squashed under a crushing weight of earth.

'Now it is all over. Now the happy home and the best of wives will welcome you no more, nor winsome children rush to snatch the first kiss at your coming and touch your heart with speechless joy. No chance now to further your fortune or safeguard your family. Unhappy man,' they cry, 'unhappily cheated by one treacherous day out of all the uncounted blessings of life!' But they do not go on to say: 'And now no repining for these lost joys will oppress you any more.' If they perceived this clearly with their minds and acted according to the words, they would free their breasts from a great load of grief and dread.

'Ah yes! *You* are at peace now in the sleep of death, and so you will stay to the end of time. Pain and sorrow will never touch you again. But to *us*, who stood weeping inconsolably while you were consumed to ashes on the dreadful pyre – to us no day will come that will lift the undying sorrow from our hearts.' Ask the speaker, then, what is so heart-rending about this. If something returns to sleep and peace, what reason is that for pining in inconsolable grief?

Here, again, is the way men often talk from the bottom of their hearts when they recline at a banquet, goblet in hand and brows decked with garlands: 'How all too short are these good times that come to us poor creatures! Soon they will be past and gone, and there will be no recalling them.' You would think the crowning calamity in store for them after death was to be parched and shrivelled by a tormenting thirst or oppressed by some other vain desire. But even in sleep, when mind and body alike are at rest, no one misses himself or sighs for life. If such sleep were prolonged to eternity, no longing for ourselves would trouble us. And yet the vital atoms in our limbs cannot be far removed from their sensory motions at a time when a mere jolt out of sleep enables a man to pull himself together. Death, therefore, must be regarded, so far as we are concerned, as having much less existence than sleep, if anything can have less existence than what we perceive to be nothing. For death is followed by a far greater dispersal of the seething mass of matter: once that icy breach in life has intervened, there is no more waking.

Suppose that Nature herself were suddenly to find a voice and round upon one of us in these terms: 'What is your grievance, mortal, that you give yourself up to this whining and repining? Why do you weep and wail over death? If the life you have lived till now has been a pleasant thing – if all its blessings have not leaked away like water poured into a cracked pot and run to waste unrelished – why then, you silly creature, do you not retire as a guest who has had his fill of life and take your care-free rest with a quiet mind? Or, if all your gains have been poured profitless away and life has grown distasteful, why do you seek to swell the total? The new can but turn out as badly as the old and perish as unprofitably. Why not rather make an end of life and labour? Do you expect me to invent some new contrivance for your pleasure? I tell you, there is none. All things are always the same. If your body is not yet withered with age, nor your limbs decrepit and flagging, even so there is nothing new to look forward to – not though you should outlive all living creatures, or even though you should never die at all.' What are we to answer, except that Nature's rebuttal is justified and the plea she puts forward is a true one?

But suppose it is some man of riper years who complains – some dismal greybeard who frets unconscionably at his approaching end. Would she not have every right to protest more vehemently and repulse him in stern tones: 'Away with your tears, old reprobate! Have done with your grumbling! You are withering now after tasting all the joys of life. But, because you are always pining for what is not and unappreciative of the things at hand, your life has slipped away unfulfilled and unprized. Death has stolen upon you unawares, before you are ready to retire from life's banquet filled and satisfied. Come now, put away all that is unbecoming to your years and compose your mind to make way for others.

You have no choice.' I cannot question but she would have right on her side; her censure and rebuke would be well merited. The old is always thrust aside to make way for the new, and one thing must be built out of the wreck of another. There is no murky pit of Hell awaiting anyone. There is need of matter, so that later generations may arise; when they have lived out their span, they will all follow you. Bygone generations have taken your road, and those to come will take it no less. So one thing will never cease to spring from another. To none is life given in freehold; to all on lease. Look back at the eternity that passed before we were born, and mark how utterly it counts to us as nothing. This is a mirror that Nature holds up to us, in which we may see the time that shall be after we are dead. Is there anything terrifying in the sight – anything depressing – anything that is not more restful than the soundest sleep?

As for all those torments that are said to take place in the depths of Hell, they are actually present here and now, in our own lives.

There is no wretched Tantalus, as the myth relates, transfixed with groundless terror at the huge boulder poised above him in the air. But in this life there really are mortals oppressed by unfounded fear of the gods and trembling at the impending doom that may fall upon any of them at the whim of chance.

There is no Tityos lying in Hell for ever probed by birds of prey. Assuredly they cannot find food by groping under those giant ribs to glut them throughout eternity. No matter to what lenght that titanic frame may lie outstretched, so that he covers not a paltry nine acres with his spread-eagled limbs but the whole extent of earth, he will not be able to suffer an eternity of pain nor furnish food from his body for evermore. But Tityos is here in our midst – that poor devil prostrated by love, torn indeed by birds of prey, devoured by gnawing jealousy or rent by the fangs of some other passion.

Sisyphus too is alive for all to see, bent on winning the insignia of office, its rods and ruthless axes, by the people's vote and embittered by perpetual defeat. To strive for this profitless and never-granted prize, and in striving toil and moil incessantly, this truly is to push a boulder laboriously up a steep hill, only to see it, once the top is reached, rolling and bounding down again to the flat levels of the plain.

By the same token, to be for ever feeding a malcontent mind, filling it with good things but never satisfying it – the fate we suffer when the circling seasons enrich us with their products and their ever-changing charms but we are never filled with the fruits of life – this surely exemplifies the story of those maidens in the flower of life for ever pouring water into a leaking vessel which can never by any sleight be filled.

As for Cerberus and the Furies and the pitchy darkness and the jaws of Hell belching abominable fumes, these are not and cannot be anywhere at all. But life is darkened by the fear of retribution for our misdeeds, a fear enormous in proportion to their enormity, and by the penalties imposed for crime – imprisonment and ghastly precipitation from Tarpeia's Crag, the lash, the block, the rack, the boiling pitch, the firebrand and the branding iron. Even though these horrors are not physically present, yet the conscience-ridden mind in terrified anticipation torments itself with its own goads and whips. It does not see what term there can be to its suffering nor where its punishment can have an end. It is afraid that death may serve merely to intensify pain. So at length the life of misguided mortals becomes a Hell on earth.

Here is something that you might well say to yourself from time to time: 'Even good king Ancus looked his last on the daylight – a better man than you, my presumptuous friend, by a long reckoning. Death has come to many another monarch and potentate, who lorded it over mighty nations. Even that King of Kings who once built a highway across the great deep – who gave his legions a path to tread among the waves and taught them to march on foot over the briny gulfs and with his chargers trampled scornfully upon the ocean's roar – even he was robbed of the light and poured out the spirit from a dying frame. Scipio, that thunderbolt of war, the terror of Carthage, gave his bones to the earth as if he had been the meanest of serfs. Add to this company the discoverers of truth and beauty. Add the attendants of the Muses, among them Homer who in solitary glory bore the sceptre but has sunk into the same slumber as the rest. Democritus, when ripe age warned him that the mindful motions of his intellect were running down, made his unbowed head a willing sacrifice to death. And the Master himself, when his daylit race was run, Epicurus himself died, whose genius outshone the race of men and dimmed them all, as the stars are dimmed by the rising of the fiery sun. And will *you* kick and protest against your sentence? You, whose life is next-door to death while you are still alive and looking on the light. You, who waste the major part of your time in sleep and, when you are awake, are snoring still and dreaming. You, who bear a mind hag-ridden by baseless fear and cannot find the commonest cause of your distress, hounded as you are, poor creature, by a pack of troubles and drifting in a drunken stupor upon a wavering tide of fantasy.'

Men feel plainly enough within their minds, a heavy burden, whose weight depresses them. If only they perceived with equal clearness the causes of this depression, the origin of this lump of evil within their breasts, they would not lead such a life as we now see all too commonly – no one knowing what he really wants and everyone for ever trying to get away from where he is, as though mere locomotion could throw off the load. Often the owner of some stately mansion, bored stiff by staying at home, takes his departure, only to return as speedily when he feels himself no better off out of doors. Off he goes to his country seat, driving his carriage and pair hot-foot, as though in haste to save a house on fire. No sooner has he crossed its doorstep than he starts yawning or retires moodily to sleep and courts oblivion, or else rushes back to revisit the city. In so doing the individual is really running away from himself. Since he remains reluctantly wedded to the self whom he cannot of course escape, he grows to hate him, because he is a sick man ignorant of the cause of his malady. If he did but see this, he would cast other thoughts aside and devote himself first to studying the nature of the universe. It is not the fortune of an hour that is in question, but of all time – the lot in store for mortals throughout the eternity that awaits them after death.

What is this deplorable lust of life that holds us trembling in bondage to such uncertainties and dangers? A fixed term is set to the life of mortals, and there is no way of dodging death. In any case the setting of our lives remains the same throughout, and by going on living we do not mint any new coin of pleasure. So long as the object of our craving is unattained, it seems more precious than anything besides. Once it is ours, we crave for something else. So an unquenchable thirst for life keeps us always on the gasp. There is no telling what fortune the future may bring – what chance may throw in our way, or what upshot lies in waiting. By prolonging life, we cannot subtract or whittle away one jot from the duration of our death. The time after our taking off remains constant. However many generations you may add to your store by living, there waits for you none the less the same eternal death. The time of not-being will be no less for him who made an end of life with yesterday's daylight than for him who perished many a moon and many a year before.

Sensation and Sex

I am blazing a trail through pathless tracts of the Muses'
Pierian realm, where no foot has ever trod before. What
joy it is to light upon virgin springs and drink their
waters. What joy to pluck new flowers and gather for
my brow a glorious garland from fields whose blossoms
were never yet wreathed by the Muses round any head.
This is my reward for teaching on these lofty topics, for
struggling to loose men's minds from the tight knots of
superstition and shedding on dark corners the bright
beam of my song that irradiates everything with the
sparkle of the Muses. My art is not without a purpose.
Physicians, when they wish to treat children with a nasty
dose of wormwood, first smear the rim of the cup with
a coat of yellow honey. The children, too young as yet
for foresight, are lured by the sweetness at their lips into
swallowing the bitter draught. So they are tricked but
not trapped; for the treatment restores them to health.
In the same way our doctrine often seems unpalatable
to those who have not sampled it, and the multitude
shrink from it. That is why I have tried to administer it
to you in the dulcet strains of poesy, coated with the
sweet honey of the Muses. My object has been to engage
your mind with my verses while you gain insight into
the nature of the universe and learn to appreciate the
profit you are reaping.

*

I have already shown what the component bodies of everything are like; how they vary in shape; how they fly spontaneously through space, impelled by a perpetual motion; and how from these all objects can be created. I have further shown what is the nature of the mind; by what forces it is brought to its full strength in union with the body; and how it is disintegrated and returns to its component atoms.

Now I will embark on an explanation of a highly relevant fact, *the existence of what we call 'images' of things*, a sort of outer skin perpetually peeled off the surface of objects and flying about this way and that through the air. It is these whose impact scares our minds, whether waking or sleeping, on those occasions when we catch a glimpse of strange shapes and phantoms of the dead. Often, when we are sunk in slumber, they startle us with the notion that spirits may get loose from Hades and ghosts hover about among the living, and that some part of us may survive after death when body and mind alike have been disintegrated and dissolved into their component atoms.

I maintain therefore that replicas or insubstantial shapes of things are thrown off from the surface of objects. These we must denote as an outer skin or film, because each particular floating image wears the aspect and form of the object from whose body it has emanated. This you may infer, however dull your wit, from the following facts.

In the first place, within the range of vision, many objects give off particles. Some of these are rarefied and diffused, such as the smoke emitted by logs or the heat by fire. Others are denser and more closely knit: cicadas, for instance, in summer periodically shed their tubular jackets; calves at birth cast off cauls from the surface of their bodies; the slippery snake sloughs off on thorns the garment we often see fluttering on a briar. Since these things happen, objects must also give off a much flimsier film from the surface of their bodies. For, since those more solid emanations fall off, no reason can be given why such flimsy ones should not. Besides, we know that on the surface of objects there are lots of tiny particles, which could be thrown off without altering the order of their arrangement or the outline of their shape, and all the faster because, being relatively few and lying right on the outside, they are less liable to obstruction.

We certainly see that many objects throw off matter in abundance, not only from their inmost depths, as we have said before, but from their surfaces in the form of colour. This is done conspicuously by the awnings, yellow, scarlet and maroon, stretched flapping and billowing on poles and rafters over spacious theatres. The crowded pit below and the stage with all its scenery are made to glow and flow with the colours of the canopy. The more completely the theatre is hemmed in by surrounding walls, the more its interior, sheltered from the daylight, is irradiated by this flood of colour. Since canvasses thus give off colour from their surface, all objects must give off filmy images as a result of spraying particles from their surfaces this way and that. Here then, already definitely established, we have indications of images, flying about everywhere, extremely fine in texture and individually invisible.

Again, the reason why smell, smoke, heat and the like come streaming out of objects in shapeless clouds is that they originate in the inmost depths; so they are split up in their circuitous journey, and there are no straight vents to their channels through which they may issue directly in close formation. When the thin film of surface colour, on the other hand, is thrown off, there is nothing to disrupt it, since it lies exposed right on the outside.

Lastly, the reflections that we see in mirrors or in water or any polished surface have the same appearance as actual objects. They must therefore be composed of films given off by those objects. There exist therefore flimsy but accurate replicas of objects, individually invisible but such that, when flung back in a rapid succession of recoils from the flat surface of mirrors they produce a visible image. That is the only conceivable way in which these films can be preserved so as to reproduce such a perfect likeness of each object.

Let me now explain *how flimsy is the texture of these films*. In the first place, the atoms themselves are vastly below the range of our senses – vastly smaller than the first objects, on a descending scale, that the eye can no longer discern. In confirmation of this, let me illustrate in a few words the minuteness of the atoms of which everything is composed. First, there are animals that are already so tiny that a third part of them would be quite invisible. How are we to picture one of the internal organs of these – the tiny globule of the heart, or the eyes? Of what size are its limbs or their joints? What must be the component atoms of its spirit and its mind? You cannot help seeing how slight and diminutive these must be. Or again, consider those substances that emit a pungent odour – all-heal, bitter wormwood, oppressive southernwood, the astringent tang of centaury. If you lightly crush one of these herbs between two fingers, the scent will cling to your hand, but its particles will be quite invisible. This will convey some notion of the number of surface-films from objects that must be flying about in a variety of ways without producing any effect on the senses. You must not suppose that the only films moving about are those that emanate from objects. *There are also films spontaneously generated* and composed in this lower region of the sky which we call the air. These assume a diversity of shapes and travel at a great height. So at times we see clouds smoothly condensing up aloft, defacing the bright aspect of the firmament and ruffling the air by their motion. Often giant faces appear to be sailing by, trailing large patches of shadow. Sometimes it seems that great mountains, or crags uprooted from mountains, are drifting by and passing over the sun. Then other clouds, black with storm, appear to be towed along in the wake of some passing monster. In their fluidity they never cease to change their form, assuming the outline now of one shape, now of another.

Let us now consider *with what facility and speed the films are generated* and ceaselessly stream out of objects and slide off their surfaces. For the outermost skin of all objects is always in readiness for them to shed. When this comes in contact with other objects, it may pass through, as it does in particular through glass. When it encounters rough rocks or solid wood, then it is promptly diffracted, so that it cannot reproduce an image. But when it is confronted by something both polished and close-grained, in particular a mirror, then neither of these things happens. The films cannot penetrate, as they do through glass; nor are they diffracted, because the smoothness ensures their preservation. That is why such surfaces reflect images that are visible to us. No matter how suddenly or at what time you set any object in front of a mirror, an image appears. From this you may infer that the surfaces of objects emit a ceaseless stream of flimsy tissues and filmy shapes. Therefore a great many films are generated in a brief space of time, so that their origin can rightly be described as instantaneous. Just as a great many particles of light must be emitted in a brief space of time by the sun to keep the world continually filled with it, so objects in general must correspondingly send off a great many images in a great many ways from every surface and in all directions instantaneously. Turn the mirror which way we will, objects are reproduced in it with corresponding shape and colour.

Again, when the weather has been most brilliant, it becomes gloomy and overcast with amazing suddenness. You would fancy that all the nether darkness from every quarter had abandoned Hades and crowded the spacious vaults of heaven: so grim a night of storm gathers aloft, from which lours down the face of black fear. In comparison with such a mass of matter, no one can express how minute a surface-film is, or convey any idea of the proportion in words.

*

Let me now explain in my verses *how speedily the films move* and what power they possess of swimming swiftly through the air, so that a brief hour is spent on a long journey, whatever course each one may pursue in response to its particular impulse. My account will be persuasive rather than exhaustive. Better the fleeting melody of the swan than the long-drawn clangour of cranes high up among the northward-racing clouds.

First then, it is a common observation that light objects and those composed of small particles are swift-moving. A notable example is the light and heat of the sun: these are composed of minute atoms which, when they are shoved off, lose no time in shooting right across the interspace of air in the direction imparted by the shove. The supply of light is promptly renewed by fresh light, and one flash is set going by another in a continuous procession. Similarly the films must be able to traverse an incalculable space in an instant of time, and that for two reasons. First, a very slight initial impetus far away to their rear sufficed to launch them and they continue on their course at a velocity proportionate to their lightness. Secondly, they are thrown off with such a loose-knit texture that they can readily penetrate any object and filter through the interspace of air.

Again certain particles thrown up to the surface from the inmost depths of objects, namely those that form the light and heat of the sun, are seen at the very instant of daybreak to drop and spray out across the whole space of the sky and fly over sea and lands and flood the firmament. What then of particles that are already lying right on the surface when they are thrown off and whose egress is not hampered by any obstacle? Surely they must go all the faster and the farther and traverse an extent of space many times as great in the time it takes for the sunlight to flash across the sky?

A further and especially convincing indication of the velocity of surface-films is this. Expose a smooth surface of water to the open sky when it is bright with stars: immediately the sparkling constellations of the firmament in all their unclouded splendour are reproduced in the water. Does not this indicate how instantaneous is the descent of the image from the border-land of ether to the borders of earth? Here then is proof upon proof that objects emit particles that strike upon the eyes and provoke sight.

From certain objects there also flows a perpetual stream of odour, as coolness flows from rivers, heat from the sun, and from the ocean waves a spray that eats away walls round the sea-shore. Sounds of every sort are surging incessantly through the air. When we walk by the seaside, a salty tang of brine enters our mouth; when we watch a draught of wormwood being mixed in our presence, a bitter effluence touches it. So from every object flows a stream of matter, spreading out in all directions. The stream must flow without rest or intermission, since our senses are perpetually alert and everything is always liable to be seen or smelt or to provoke sensation by sound.

Again, when some shape or other is handled in the dark, it is recognized as the same shape that in a clear and shining light is plain to see. It follows that *touch and sight are provoked by the same stimulus.* Suppose we touch a square object and it stimulates our sense in the dark. What can it be that, given light, will strike upon our vision as square, if it is not the film emanating from the object? This shows that the cause of seeing lies in these films and without these nothing can be seen.

It is established, then, that these films, as I call them, are moving about everywhere, sprayed and scattered in all directions. Since we can see only with our eyes, we have only to direct our vision towards any particular quarter for all the objects there to strike it with their shapes and colours. Our power of perceiving and distinguishing the distance from us of each particular object is also due to the film. For, as soon as it is thrown off, it shoves and drives before it all the air that intervenes between itself and the eyes. All this air flows through our eyeballs and brushes through our pupils in passing. That is how we perceive the distance of each object: the more air is driven in front of the film and the longer the draught that brushes through our eyes, the more remote the object is seen to be. Of course this all happens so quickly that we perceive the nature of the object and its distance simultaneously.

It need occasion no surprise that, while the individual films that strike upon the eye are invisible, the objects from which they emanate are perceived. Wind too buffets us in driblets, and cold strikes us in a piercing stream; yet we do not feel each particular unit of the wind or the cold, but simply the total effect. And we see that blows are then being delivered on our body with an effect as though some external object were buffeting it and producing the sensation of its bodily presence. When we hit a stone with our toe, what we actually touch is only the outer surface of the rock, the overlying film of colour; but what we feel ourselves touching is not that but the hard inner core of the rock.

Let us now consider *why the image is seen beyond the mirror* – for it certainly does appear to be some distance behind the surface. It is just as though we were really looking out through a doorway, when the door offers a free prospect through it and affords a glimpse of many objects outside the house. In this case also the vision is accompanied by a double dose of air. First we perceive the air within the door posts; then follow the posts themselves to right and left; then the light outside and a second stretch of air brushes through the eyes, followed by the objects that are really seen out of doors. A similar thing happens when a mirrored image projects itself upon our sight. On its way to us the film shoves and drives before it all the air that intervenes between itself and the eyes, so that we feel all this before perceiving the mirror. When we have perceived the mirror itself, then the film that travels from us to it and is reflected comes back to our eyes, pushing another lot of air in front of it, so that we perceive this before the image, which thus appears to lie at some distance from the mirror. Here then is ample reason why we should not be surprised at this appearance of objects reflected in the surface of a mirror, since they involve a double journey with two lots of air.

*

Now for the question *why our right side appears in mirrors on the left*. The reason is that, when the film on its outward journey strikes the flat surface of a mirror, it is not slewed round intact, but flung straight back in reverse. It is just as if someone were to take a plaster mask before it had set and hurl it against a pillar or beam, so that it bounced straight back, preserving the features imprinted on its front but displaying them now in reverse. In this case what had been the right eye would now be the left and the left correspondingly would have become the right.

It may also happen that a film is passed on from one mirror to another, so that as many as five or six images are produced. Objects tucked away in the inner part of a house, however long and winding the approach to their hiding place, can thus be brought into sight along devious routes by a series of mirrors. So the image is flashed from mirror to mirror. And on each occasion what is transmitted as the left becomes the right and is then again reversed and returns to its original relative position.

Again, mirrors with projecting sides whose curvature matches our own give back to us unreversed images. This may be because the film is thrown from one surface of the mirror to the other and reaches us only after a double rebound. Alternatively, it may be that on reaching the mirror the film is slewed round, because the curved surface gives it a twist towards us.

You would fancy that images walk along with us, keeping step and copying our gestures. This is because, as soon as you withdraw from a bit of the mirror, no films can be reflected from that part. Nature ordains that every particle shall rebound from the reflecting surface at an angle corresponding to its incidence.

Now for the fact that *the eyes avoid bright objects* and refuse to gaze at them. The sun, indeed, actually blinds them if you persist in directing them towards it. The reason is that its force is immense and the films it gives off travel with great momentum through a great depth of pure air and hit the eyes hard, so as to disrupt their atomic structure. Besides, a bright light that is painful often scorches the eyes, because it contains many particles of fire whose infiltration sets them smarting.

Sufferers from jaundice, again, *see everything they look at as yellow.* This is because many particles of yellowness from their own bodies are streaming out in the path of the approaching films. There are also many such particles blended in the structure of their own eyes, and by contamination with these everything is sullied with their sallowness.

When we are in the dark we see objects that are in the light for the following reason. The black murky air that lies nearer to us enters first into our open eyes and takes possession of them. It is then closely followed by bright and shining air, which cleanses them and dispels the shadows of the earlier air. For the bright air is many degrees more mobile and many degrees finer-grained and more potent. As soon as this has filled the passages of the eyes with light and opened those that had previously been blockaded by dark air, they are immediately followed by films thrown off from the illuminated objects, and these stimulate our sense of sight. On the other hand, when we look out of light into darkness, we can see nothing: the murky air, of muddier consistency, arrives last and chokes all the inlets of the eyes and blockades their passages, so that they cannot be stirred by the impact of films from any object.

When we see the square towers of a city in the distance, they often appear round. This is because every angle seen at a distance is blunted or even is not seen as an angle at all. Its impact is nullified and does not penetrate as far as our eyes, because films that travel through a great deal of air lose their sharp outlines through frequent collisions with it. When every angle has thus eluded our sense, the result is as though the squared ashlars were rounded off on the lathe – not that they resemble really round stones seen close up, but in a sketchy sort of way they counterfeit them.

Again, *our shadow in the sunlight seems to us to move* and keep step with us and imitate our gestures, incredible though it is that unillumined air should walk about in conformity with a man's movements and gestures. For what we commonly call a shadow can be nothing but air deprived of light. Actually the earth is robbed of sunlight in a definite succession of places wherever it is obstructed by us in our progression, and the part we have left is correspondingly replenished with it. That is why the successive shadows of our body seem to be the same shadow following us along steadily step by step.

New particles of radiance are always streaming down and their predecessors are consumed, as the saying goes, like wool being spun into the fire. So the earth is easily robbed of light and is correspondingly replenished and washes off the black stains of shadow.

Here, as always, *we do not admit that the eyes are in any way deluded*. It is their function to see where light is, and where shadow. But whether one light is the same as another, and whether the shadow that was here is moving over there, or whether on the other hand what really happens is what I have just described – that is something to be discerned by the reasoning power of the mind. The nature of phenomena cannot be understood by the eyes. You must not hold them responsible for this fault of the mind.

A ship in which we are sailing is on the move, though it seems to stand still. Another that rides at anchor gives the impression of sailing by. Hills and plains appear to be drifting astern when our ship soars past them with sails for wings.

The stars all seem motionless, embedded in the ethereal vault; yet they must all be in constant motion, since they rise and traverse the heavens with their luminous bodies till they return to the far-off scene of their setting. So too the sun and moon appear to remain at their posts, though the facts prove them travellers.

Mountains rising from the midst of the sea in the far distance, though there may be ample space between them for the free passage of a fleet, look as if linked together in a single island.

When children have come to a standstill after spinning

round, they seem to see halls and pillars whirling round them – and so vividly that they can scarcely believe that the whole roof is not threatening to tumble on top of them.

When nature is just beginning to fling up the light of day, ruddy with flickering fires, and lift it high above the hill-tops, the glowing sun seems to perch upon the hills and kindle them by direct contact with its own fire. Yet these same hills are distant from us a bare two thousand bowshots – often indeed no more than five hundred javelin casts. But between hills and sun lie enormous tracts of ocean, overarched by vast ethereal vaults, and many thousand intervening lands, peopled by all the various races of men and beasts.

A puddle no deeper than a finger's breadth, formed in a hollow between the cobble-stones of the highway, offers to the eye a downward view, below the ground, of as wide a scope as the towering immensity of sky that yawns above. You would fancy you saw clouds far down below you and a sky and heavenly bodies deep-buried in a miraculous heaven beneath the earth.

When the mettlesome steed we are riding stands stock-still in midstream and we glance down at the swift-flowing torrent, our stationary mount seems to be breasting the flood and forcing its way rapidly upstream; and, wherever we cast our eyes, everything seems to be surging and forging ahead with the same movement as ourselves.

When we gaze from one end down the whole length of a colonnade, though its structure is perfectly symmetrical and it is propped throughout on pillars of equal height, yet it contracts by slow degrees in a narrowing cone that draws roof to floor and left to right till it unites them in the imperceptible apex of the cone.

To sailors at sea, the sun appears to rise out of the waves and to set in the waves and there hide its light. This is because they do in fact see only water and sky – another warning not to jump to the conclusion that the senses are shaky guides on all points.

To landsmen ignorant of the sea, ships in harbour seem to be riding crippled on the waves, with their poops broken. So much of the oars as projects above the waterline is straight, and so is the upper part of the rudder. But all the submerged parts appear refracted and wrenched round in an upward direction and almost as though bent right back so as to float on the surface.

At a time when scattered clouds are scudding before the wind across the night sky, the sparkling constellations look as though they were gliding along in the teeth of the clouds and passing overhead in a direction quite different from their actual course.

If we press our hand against one eye from below, a new sort of perception results. Whatever we look at, we see double: the lamplight, aflower with flame, becomes twin lights; the furniture throughout the house is doubled; men wear double faces and two bodies apiece.

When sleep has fettered all our limbs in the pleasant chains of slumber, and the whole body has sunk in utter tranquillity, we still seem to ourselves to be wide awake and moving our limbs. In the pitch blackness of night we fancy ourselves gazing on the sun and the broad light of day. In a confined space, we seem to traverse sky and sea, rivers and mountains, and wander afoot over prairies. With the solemn hush of night all around, we listen to sounds; we speak aloud without a word uttered.

We have many other paradoxical experiences of the same kind, all of which seem bent on shaking our faith in the senses. But all to no purpose. Most of this illusion is due to the mental assumptions which we ourselves superimpose, so that things not perceived by the senses pass for perceptions. There is nothing harder than to separate the facts as revealed from the questionable interpretations promptly imposed on them by the mind.

If anyone thinks that nothing can be known, he does not know whether even this can be known, since he admits that he knows nothing. Against such an adversary, therefore, who deliberately stands on his head, I will not trouble to argue my case. And yet, if I were to grant that he possessed this knowledge, I might ask several pertinent questions. Since he has had no experience of truth, how does he know the difference between knowledge and ignorance? What has originated the concept of truth and falsehood? Where is his proof that doubt is not the same as certainty?

You will find, in fact, that the concept of truth was originated by the senses and that the senses cannot be rebutted. The testimony that we must accept as more trustworthy is that which can spontaneously overcome falsehood with truth. What then are we to pronounce more trustworthy than the senses? Can reason derived from the deceitful senses be invoked to contradict them, when it is itself wholly derived from the senses? If they are not true, then reason in its entirety is equally false. Or can hearing give the lie to sight, or touch to hearing? Can touch in turn be discredited by taste or refuted by the nostrils or rebutted by the eyes? This, in my view, is out of the question. Each sense has its own distinctive faculty, its specific function. There must be separate discernment of softness and cold and heat and of the various colours of things and whatever goes with the colours; separate functioning of the palate's power of taste; separate generation of scents and sounds. This rules out the possibility of one sense confuting another. It will be equally out of the question for one sense to belie itself, since it will always be entitled to the same degree of credence. Whatever the senses may perceive at any time is all alike true. Suppose that reason cannot elucidate the cause why things that were square when close at hand are seen as round in the distance. Even so, it is better, in default of reason, to assign fictitious causes to the two shapes than to let things clearly apprehended slip from our grasp. This is to attack belief at its very roots – to tear up the entire foundation on which the maintenance of life is built. It is not only reason that would collapse completely. If you did not dare trust your senses so as to keep clear of precipices and other such things to be avoided and make for their opposites, there would be a speedy end to life itself.

So all this armament that you have marshalled against the senses is nothing but a futile array of words. If you set out to construct a building with a crooked ruler, a faulty square that is set a little out of the straight and a level ever so slightly askew, there can be only one outcome – a crazy, rickety, higgledy-piggledy huddle, sagging here and bulging there, with bits that look like falling at any moment and all in fact destined to fall, doomed by the initial miscalculations on which the structure is based. Just as rickety and just as defective must be the structure of your reasoning, if the senses on which it rests are themselves deceptive.

After this the problem that next confronts us – to determine *how each of the remaining senses perceives its own objects* – is not a particularly thorny one.

In the first place, all forms of *sound and vocal utterance* become audible when they have slipped into the ear and provoked sensation by the impact of their own bodies. The fact that voices and other sounds can impinge on the senses is itself a proof of their corporeal nature. Besides, the voice often scrapes the throat and a shout roughens the windpipe on its outward path. What happens is that, when atoms of voice in greater numbers than usual have begun to squeeze out through the narrow outlet, the doorway of the overcrowded mouth gets scraped. Undoubtedly, if voices and words have this power of causing pain, they must consist of corporeal particles. Again, you must have noticed how much it takes out of a man, and what wear and tear it causes to his thews and sinews, to keep on talking from the first glow of dawn till the evening shadows darken, especially if his words are uttered at the pitch of his voice. Since much talking actually takes something out of the body, it follows that voice is composed of bodily stuff. Finally, the harshness of a sound is due to the harshness of its component atoms, and its smoothness to their smoothness. There is a marked difference in the shape of the atoms that enter our ears when a low-toned trumpet booms its *basso profondo* and the hoarse-throated roar re-echoes from savage crags, and when the swans' plaintive dirge floats up in doleful melody from the winding glens of Helicon.

When we force out these utterances from the depths of our body and launch them through the direct outlet of the mouth, they are cut up into lengths by the flexible tongue, the craftsman of words, and moulded in turn by the configuration of the lips. At a point reached by each particular utterance after travelling no great distance from its source, it naturally happens that the individual words are also clearly audible and distinguishable syllable by syllable. For the utterance preserves its shape and configuration. But if the intervening space is unduly wide, the words must inevitably be jumbled and the utterance disjointed by its flight through a long stretch of gusty air. So it happens that, while you are aware of a sound, you cannot discern the sense of the words: the utterance comes to you so muddled and entangled.

If often happens that a single word, uttered from the mouth of a crier, penetrates the ears of a whole crowd. Evidently, a single utterance must split up immediately into a multitude of utterances, since it is parcelled out among a number of separate ears, imprinting upon each the shape of a word and its distinctive sound. Such of these utterances as do not strike upon the ears float by and are scattered to the winds and lost without effect. Some of them, however, bump against solid objects and bounce back, so as to carry back a sound and sometimes mislead with the replica of a word. Once you have grasped this, you can explain to yourself and to others how it is that in desert places, when we are searching for comrades who have scattered and strayed among overshadowed glens and hail them at the pitch of our voices, the cliffs fling back the forms of our words in due sequence. I have observed places tossing back six or seven utterances when you have launched a single one: with their tendency to rebound, the words were reverberated and reiterated from hill to hill. According to local legend, these places are haunted by goat-footed Satyrs and by Nymphs. Tales are told of Fauns, whose noisy revels and merry pranks shatter the mute hush of night for miles around; of twanging lyre-strings and plaintive melodies poured out by flutes at the touch of the players' finger; of music far-heard by the country-folk when Pan, tossing the pine-branches that wreathe his brutish head, runs his arched lips again and again along the wind-mouthed reeds, so that the pipe's wildwood rhapsody flows on unbroken. Many such fantasies and fairly tales are related by the rustics. Perhaps, in boasting of these marvels, they hope to dispel the notion that they live in backwoods abandoned even by the gods. Perhaps they have some other motive, since mankind everywhere has greedy ears for such romancing.

There remains the problem, not a very puzzling one, of how sounds can penetrate and strike on the ear through media through which objects cannot be clearly perceived by the eye. The obvious reason why we often see a conversation going on through closed doors is that an utterance can make its way intact through circuitous fissures in objects impervious to visual films. For these are broken up, unless they are passing through straight fissures such as those in glass, which is penetrable by any sort of image. Again, sounds are disseminated in all directions because each one, after its initial splintering into a great many parts, gives birth to others, just as a spark of fire often propagates itself by starting fires of its own. So places out of the direct path are often filled with voices, which surge round every obstacle, one sound being provoked by another. But visual films all continue in straight lines along their initial paths, so that no one can see over a wall, as he can hear voices from inside it. Even a voice, however, is blunted in its passage through barriers and reaches our ears blurred, so that we seem to hear a mere noise rather than words.

As for the organs of *taste*, the tongue and the palate, they do not call for lengthier explanation or more expenditure of labour. In the first place, we perceive taste in the mouth when we squeeze it out by chewing food, just as if someone were to grasp a sponge full of water in his hand and begin to squeeze it dry. Next, all that we squeeze out is diffused through the pores of the palate and the winding channels of the spongy tongue. When the trickling particles of savour are smooth, they affect the palate pleasantly and pleasantly tickle all the moist regions of the tongue in their circuitous flow. Others, in proportion as their shape is rougher, tend more to prick and tear the organs of sense by their entry.

The pleasure derived from taste does not extend

beyond the palate. When the tasty morsel has all been gulped down the gullet and is being distributed through the limbs, it gives no more pleasure. It does not matter a rap what food you take to nourish your body so long as you can digest it and distribute it through your limbs and preserve the right balance of fluid in the stomach.

Let me now explain why one man's meat is not another's, and what is bitter and unpalatable to one may strike another as highly agreeable. The difference in reaction is indeed so great that what is food to one may be literally poison to others. There is, for instance, a snake that is so affected by contact with human spittle that it bites itself to death. To us hellebore is rank poison; but goats and quails grow fat on it. In order to understand how this happens, the first point to remember is one that I have already mentioned, the diversity of atoms that are commingled in objects. With the outward differences between the various types of animal that take food – the specific distinctions revealed by the external contour of their limbs – there go corresponding differences in the shapes of their component atoms. These in their turn entail differences in the chinks and channels – the pores, as we call them – in all parts of the body, including the mouth and the palate itself. In some species these are naturally smaller, in others larger; in some triangular, in others square; while many are round, others are of various polygonal shapes. In short, the shapes and motions of the atoms rigidly determine the shapes of the pores: the atomic structure defines the interatomic channels. When something sweet to one is bitter to another, it must be because its smoothest particles palpably penetrate the palate of the former, whereas the latter's gullet is evidently invaded by particles that are rough and jagged. On this basis the whole problem becomes easily soluble. Thus, when some person is afflicted with fever through superfluity of bile, or sickness is provoked in him by some other factor, his entire body is simultaneously upset and all the positions of the component atoms are changed. It follows that particles which used to be conformable to the channels of his sense are so no longer, whereas an easier ingress is afforded to those other particles whose entry can provoke a disagreeable sensation. For, as I have already demonstrated many times, the flavour of honey actually consists of a mixture of both kinds, pleasant and unpleasant.

Let me now tackle the question *how the nostrils are affected by the impact of smell*.

First, then, there must be a multitude of objects giving off a multifarious effluence of smells, which is to be conceived as emitted in a stream and widely diffused. But particular smells, owing to their distinctive shapes, are better adapted to particular species of animals. Bees are attracted for unlimited distances through the air by the smell of honey, vultures by carcasses. Where the cloven hoof of wild game has planted its spoor, the hunter is guided by his vanguard of hounds. The scent of man is detected far in advance by that lily-white guardian of Romulus' citadel, the goose. So each by its own particular gift of smell is attracted to its proper food or repelled from noxious poison; and thus the various species are preserved.

This specific adaptability is not confined to smells and tastes. The visible forms and colours of things are not all equally conformable to the sense organs of all species, but in some cases particular sights act rather as irritants. The sight of a cock, that herald of the dawn who banishes the night with clapping wings and lusty crowing, is intolerable to ravening lions. At the first glimpse they think only of flight. The reason is, of course, that the cock's body contains certain atoms which, when they get into the lion's eyes, prick the eyeballs and cause acute pain, so that even their bold spirits cannot long endure it. But these atoms have no power to hurt our eyes, either because they never get in at all or because, once in, they have a clear way out, so that they do not hurt the eyeball by meeting obstruction at any point.

To return to the smells that assail our nostrils, it is clear that some of them have a longer range than others. None of them, however, travels as far as voices or other sounds, not to speak of the films that strike the eyeballs and provoke sight. For smell is a straggling and tardy traveller and fades away before arriving, by the gradual dissipation of its flimsy substance into the gusty air. One reason for this is that smell originates in the depths of objects and is thus given off haltingly: an indication that odours thus seep out and escape from the inner core of objects is the fact that everything smells more strongly when broken or crushed or dissolved by fire. A further reason is that smell is evidently composed of larger atoms than sound, since it does not pass through stone walls which are readily permeable by voices and other sounds. That is why you will not find it so easy to locate the source of a smell as of a sound. The effluence grows cold by dawdling through the air and does not rush with its tidings to the senses hotfoot from its source. So it is that hounds are often at fault and have to cast round for the scent.

Let me now explain briefly *what it is that stimulates the imagination and where those images come from that enter the mind.*

My first point is this. There are a great many flimsy films from the surface of objects flying about in a great many ways in all directions. When these encounter one another in the air, they easily amalgamate, like gossamer or gold-leaf. In comparison with those films that take possession of the eye and provoke sight, these are certainly of a much flimsier texture, since they penetrate through the chinks of the body and set in motion the delicate substance of the mind within and there provoke sensation. So it is that we see the composite shapes of Centaurs and Mermaids and dogs with as many heads as Cerberus, and phantoms of the dead whose bones lie in the embrace of earth. The fact is that the films flying about everywhere are of all sorts: some are produced spontaneously in the air itself; others are derived from various objects and composed by the amalgamation of their shapes. The image of a Centaur, for instance, is certainly not formed from the life, since no living creature of this sort ever existed. But, as I have just explained, where surface films from a horse and a man accidentally come into contact, they may easily stick together on the spot, because of the delicacy and flimsiness of their texture. So also with other such chimerical creatures. Since, as I have shown above, these delicate films move with the utmost nimbleness and mobility, any one of them may easily set our mind in motion with a single touch; for the mind itself is delicate and marvellously mobile.

The truth of this explanation may be easily inferred from the following facts. First, in so far as a vision beheld by the mind closely resembles one beheld by the eye, the two must have been created in a similar fashion. Now, I have shown that I see a lion, for example, through the impact of films on the eyes. It follows that something similar accounts for the motion of the mind, which also, no less than the eyes, beholds a lion or whatever it may be by means of films. The only difference is that the objects of its vision are flimsier.

Again, when our limbs are relaxed in slumber, our mind is as wakeful as ever. The same sort of films impinge upon it then as when we are awake, but now with such vividness that in sleep we may even be convinced that we are seeing someone who has passed from life into the clutches of death and earth. This results quite naturally from the stoppage and quiescence of all the bodily senses throughout the frame, so that they cannot refute a false impression by true ones. The memory also is put out of action by sleep and does not protest that the person whom the mind fancies it sees alive has long since fallen into the power of death and dissolution. It is not surprising that dream images should move about with measured gestures of their arms and other limbs. When this happens, it means that one film has passed and is succeeded by another formed in a different posture, so that it seems as though the earlier image had changed its attitude. We must picture this succession as taking place at high speed: the films fly so quickly and are drawn from so many sources, and at any perceptible instant of time there are so many atoms to keep up the supply.

This subject raises various questions that we must elucidate if we wish to give a clear account of it.

The first question is this: Why is it that, as soon as the mind takes a fancy to think about some particular object, it promptly does so? Are we to suppose that images are waiting on our will, so that we have only to wish and the appropriate film immediately impinges on our mind, whether it be the sea that we fancy or the earth or the sky? Assemblages of men, processions, banquets, battles – does nature create all these at a word and make them ready for us? And we must remember that, at the same time and in the same place, the minds of others are contemplating utterly different objects.

Again, when in our dreams we see images walking with measured step and moving their supple limbs, why do they swing their supple arms in time with alternate legs and perform repeated movements with their feet appropriate to their shifting glances? Are we to suppose the stray films are imbued with art and trained to spend their nights in dancing?

Another answer can be given to both questions that is surely nearer the truth. In one perceptible instant of time, that is, the time required to utter a single syllable, there are many unperceived units of time whose existence is recognized by reason. That explains why, at any given time, every sort of film is ready to hand in every place: they fly so quickly and are drawn from so many sources. And, because they are so flimsy, the mind cannot distinctly perceive any but those it makes an effort to perceive. All the rest pass without effect, leaving only those for which the mind has prepared itself. And the mind prepares itself in the expectation of seeing each appearance followed by its natural sequel. So this, in fact, is what it does see. You must have noticed how even our eyes, when they set out to look at inconspicuous objects, make an effort and prepare themselves; otherwise it is not possible for us to perceive distinctly. And, even when you are dealing with visible objects, you will find that, unless you direct your mind towards them, they have about them all the time an air of detachment and remoteness. What wonder, then, if the mind misses every impression except those to which it surrenders itself? The result is that we draw sweeping conclusions from trifling indications and lead ourselves into pitfalls of delusion.

Sometimes it happens that an image is not forthcoming to match our expectation: what was a woman seems to be suddenly transformed into a man before our eyes, or we are confronted by some swift change of feature or age. Any surprise we might feel at this is checked by drowsy forgetfulness.

In this context, there is one illusion that you must do your level best to escape – an error to guard against with all your foresight. You must not imagine that the bright orbs of our eyes were created purposely, so that we might be able to look before us; that our need to stride ahead determined our equipment with the pliant props of thigh and ankle, set in the firm foundation of our feet; that our arms were fitted to stout shoulders, and helpful hands attached at either side, in order that we might do what is needful to sustain life. To interpret these or any other phenomena on these lines is perversely to turn the truth upside down. In fact, *nothing in our bodies was born in order that we might be able to use it, but the thing born creates the use.* There was no seeing before eyes were born, no talking before the tongue was created. The origin of the tongue was far anterior to speech. The ears were created long before a sound was heard. All the limbs, I am well assured, existed before their use. They cannot, therefore, have grown for the sake of being used.

Battles were fought hand to hand, limbs were mangled and bodies fouled with blood long before flashing spears were hurled. Wounds were parried at the bidding of nature before the left arm interposed a shield through the agency of art. Yes, and laying the weary frame to rest is an earlier institution than spreading comfortable beds, and thirst was quenched before ever cups were thought of. We can believe, therefore, that these instruments, whose invention sprang from need and life, have been designed to serve a purpose. Quite different are those organs that were first born themselves and afterwards provided a mental picture of their own functioning. And prominent in this latter class we find our sense-organs and bodily members. Here, then, is proof upon proof that you must banish the belief that they could have been created for the purpose of performing particular functions.

Another fact that need occasion no surprise is that *the body of every living creature by its own nature seeks after food*. I have already shown that countless particles in countless ways are passing off in a stream from all objects. But the greatest number of all must be emitted by animals. Since animals are always on the move, they lose a great many atoms, some squeezed out from the inner depths by the process of perspiration, some breathed out through the mouth when they gasp and pant. By these processes the body's density is diminished and its substance sapped. This results in pain. Hence food is taken so that, when duly distributed through limbs and veins, it may underpin the frame and rebuild its strength and sate its open-mouthed lust for eating. Moisture is similarly diffused into all the members that demand moisture; and the many accumulated particles of heat that inflame our stomach are dispelled by the advent of the fluid and quenched like a fire, so that the frame is no longer parched by burning drought. So it is that the thirst that sets you gasping is swilled out of the body and the craving of hunger glutted.

Let me now explain *how it comes about that we can stride forward at will and are empowered to move our limbs* in various ways, and what it is that has learnt to lift along this heavy load of our body. I count on you to mark my words. I will begin by repeating my previous statement that images of walking come to our mind and impinge upon it. Hence comes the will. For no one ever initiates any action without the mind first foreseeing what it wills. What it foresees is the substance of the image. So the mind, when the motions it experiences are such that it wishes to step forward, immediately jogs the vital spirit diffused through every limb and organ of the body. This is easily done, since mind and spirit are interconnected. The spirit in turn then jogs the body. And so bit by bit the whole bulk is pushed forward and set in motion.

A further effect is that the body grows less dense. The opened pores admit air, as is natural, since this is always highly mobile. The air rushes in in a stream and is thus diffused into every part of the body, however small. From the combination of these two factors it results that the body is pushed along, just as a ship is propelled by the combined action of wind and sails.

There is no need to be surprised that bodies so minute can twist round a body of such bulk and divert the course of our whole weight. The wind is tenuous enough, and its particles are diminutive; but it shoves along the mighty mass of a mighty ship, and, however much way it has gathered, a single hand steers it – a single tiller twists it this way or that. And many a heavy load is shifted and hoisted with an easy swing by a derrick, with the aid of pulleys and winches.

And now for *the problem of sleep*: by what contrivance does it flood our limbs with peace and unravel from our breasts the mind's disquietude? My answer will be persuasive rather than exhaustive: better the fleeting melody of the swan than the long-drawn clangour of cranes high up among the northward-facing clouds. It rests with you to lend an unresisting ear and an inquiring mind. Otherwise you may refuse to accept my explanation as possible and walk away with a mind that flings back the truth, though the blame lies with your own blindness.

In the first place, sleep occurs when the vital spirit throughout the body is discomposed: when part of it has been forced out and lost, part compressed and driven into the inner depths. At such times the limbs are unknit and grow limp. For undoubtedly the sensibility that is in us is caused by the spirit. When sensation is deadened by sleep, we must suppose that this is due to the derangement of the spirit or its expulsion. But it is not all expelled, or else the body would be steeped in the everlasting chill of death. If there were really no lurking particle of spirit left in the limbs, as smothered fire lurks in a heap of ashes, from what source could sentience be suddenly rekindled in the limbs, as flame leaps up from hidden fire? I will explain how this change is brought about and how the spirit can be deranged and the body grow limp. You must see to it that I do not waste my words on the wind.

First, then, a body on its outer surface borders on the gusty air and is touched by it. It must therefore be pelted by it with a continual rain of blows. That is why almost all bodies are covered with hide or shell, rind or bark. In bodies that breathe, the interior also is battered by air as it is inhaled and exhaled. Since our body is thus bombarded outside and in and the blows penetrate through little pores to its primary parts and primal elements, our limbs are subject in a sense to a gradual crumbling. The atoms of body and mind are dislodged from their stations. The result is that part of the spirit is forced out; part becomes tucked away in the interior; part is loosely scattered throughout the limbs, so that it cannot unite or engage in interacting motions, because nature interposes obstacles to combination and movement. This deep-seated change in motion means the withdrawal of sentience. At the same time, since there is some lack of matter to support the frame, the body grows weak; all the limbs slacken; arms and eyelids droop; often, when a man is seeking rest, his knees lose their strength and give way under him.

Food, again, induces sleepiness, because its action, when it is being distributed through all the veins, is the same as that of air. The heaviest kind of sleep is that which ensues on satiety or exhaustion, since it is then that the atoms are thrown into the greatest confusion under stress of their heavy labour. The same cause makes the partial congestion of spirit more deep-seated and the evacuation more extensive, and aggravates the internal separation and dislocation.

Whatever employment has the strongest hold on our interest or has last filled our waking hours, so as to engage the mind's attention, that is what seems most often to keep us occupied in sleep. Lawyers argue cases and frame contracts. Generals lead their troops into action. Sailors continue their pitched battle with the winds. And as for me, I go on with my task, for ever exploring the nature of the universe and setting down my discoveries in my native tongue. The same principle generally applies when other crafts and occupations are observed to beguile men's minds in sleep.

Similarly when men have devoted themselves whole-heartedly for days on end to entertainments, we usually find that the objects that have ceased to engage the senses have left wide open channels in the mind for the entry of their own images. So for many days the same sights hover before their eyes: even when awake, they seem to see figures dancing and swaying supple limbs; to fill their ears with the liquid melody and speaking notes of the lyre, and to watch the same crowded theatre, its stage ablaze with many-tinted splendour.

Such is the striking effect of interest and pleasure and customary employment, and not on men only but on all animals. You will see mettlesome steeds, when their limbs are at rest, still continuing in sleep to sweat and pant as if straining all their strength to win the palm, or as if the lifted barriers of the starting-post had just released them. And the huntsman's hounds, while wrapped in gentle slumber, often toss their legs with a quick jerk and utter sudden whines and draw rapid breaths of air into their nostrils as if they were hot on a newly-found scent. Even when awake, they often chase after shadowy images of stags, as though they saw them in full flight, till they shake off the illusion and return to themselves. A litter of good-tempered house-bred puppies are all agog to wriggle their bodies and heave them from the ground, just as if they were seeing the forms and faces of strangers. The fiercer the breed, the more savage must be their behaviour in sleep. The various races of birds take to flight and startle the groves of the gods at dead of night with a sudden whirr of wings. Doubtless their restful slumber is disturbed by visions of hawks swooping to the fray in fierce pursuit.

Very similar as a rule is the behaviour in sleep of human minds, whose massive motions are proportioned to massive effect. Kings take cities by storm, are themselves taken captive, join in battle and cry aloud as though they felt the assassin's dagger – and all without stirring from the spot. There are many who fight for their lives, giving vent to their agony in groans or filling the night with piercing screams as though they were writhing in the jaws of a panther or a ravening lion. Many talk in their sleep about matters of great moment and have often betrayed their own guilt. Many meet their death. Many, who feel themselves hurled bodily down to earth from towering crags, are startled out of sleep; like men who have lost their wits, they are slow in returning to themselves, so shaken are they by the tumult of their body. The thirsty man finds himself seated beside a river or a delectable spring and is near to gulping down the whole stream. Little boys often fancy when fast asleep that they are standing at a lavatory or a chamber pot and lifting up their clothes. Then they discharge all the filtered fluid of their body, and even the costly splendour of oriental coverlets does not escape a soaking. Those on the verge of manhood, in whose limbs the seed created by maturing age is beginning to gather, are invaded from without by images emanating from various bodies with tidings of an alluring face and a delightful complexion. This stimulates the organs swollen with an accumulation of seed. Often, as though their function were actually fulfilled, they discharge a flood of fluid and drench their covering.

In this last case, as I have explained, the thing in us that responds to the stimulus is the seed that comes with ripening years and strengthening limbs. For different things respond to different stimuli or provocations. *The one stimulus that evokes human seed from the human body is a human form.* As soon as this seed is dislodged from its resting-place, it travels through every member of the body, concentrating at certain reservoirs in the loins, and promptly acts upon the generative organs. These organs are stimulated and swollen by the seed. Hence follows the will to eject it in the direction in which tyrannical lust is tugging. The body makes for the source from which the mind is pierced by love. For the wounded normally fall in the direction of their wound: the blood spurts out towards the source of the blow; and the enemy who delivered it, if he is fighting at close quarters, is bespattered by the crimson stream. So, when a man is pierced by the shafts of Venus, whether they are launched by a lad with womanish limbs or a woman radiating love from her whole body, he strives towards the source of the wound and craves to be united with it and to transmit something of his own substance from body to body. His speechless yearning is a presentiment of bliss.

This, then, is what we term Venus. This is the origin of the thing called love – that drop of Venus' honey that first drips into our heart, to be followed by numbing heart-ache. Though the object of your love may be absent, images of it still haunt you and the beloved name chimes sweetly in your ears. If you find yourself thus passionately enamoured of an individual, you should keep well away from such images. Thrust from you anything that might feed your passion, and turn your mind elsewhere. Vent the seed of love upon other objects. By clinging to it you assure yourself the certainty of heart-sickness and pain. With nourishment the festering sore quickens and strengthens. Day by day the frenzy heightens and the grief deepens. Your only remedy is to lance the first wound with new incisions; to salve it, while it is still fresh, with promiscuous attachments; to guide the motions of your mind into some other channel.

Do not think that by avoiding grand passions you are missing the delights of Venus. Rather, you are reaping such profits as carry with them no penalty. Rest assured that this pleasure is enjoyed in a purer form by the healthy than by the love-sick. Lovers' passion is storm-tossed, even in the moment of fruition, by waves of delusion and incertitude. They cannot make up their mind what to enjoy first with eye or hand. They clasp the object of their longing so tightly that the embrace is painful. They kiss so fiercely that teeth are driven into lips. All this because their pleasure is not pure, but they are goaded by an underlying impulse to hurt the thing, whatever it may be, that gives rise to these budding shoots of madness.

In the actual presence of love Venus lightens the penalties she imposes, and her sting is assuaged by an admixture of alluring pleasure. For in love there is the hope that the flame of passion may be quenched by the same body that kindled it. But this runs clean counter to the course of nature. This is the one thing of which the more we have, the more our breast burns with the evil lust of having. Food and fluid are taken into our body; since they can fill their allotted places, the desire for meat and drink is thus easily appeased. But a pretty face or a pleasing complexion gives the body nothing to enjoy but insubstantial images, which all too often fond hope scatters to the winds.

When a thirsty man tries to drink in his dreams but is given no drop to quench the fire in his limbs, he clutches at images of water with fruitless effort and while he laps up a rushing stream he remains thirsty in the midst. Just so in the midst of love Venus teases lovers with images. They cannot glut their eyes by gazing on the beloved form, however closely. Their hands glean nothing from those dainty limbs in their aimless roving over all the body. Then comes the moment when with limbs entwined they pluck the flower of youth. Their bodies thrill with the presentiment of joy, and it is seed-time in the fields of Venus. Body clings greedily to body; moist lips are pressed on lips, and deep breaths are drawn through clenched teeth. But all to no purpose. One can glean nothing from the other, nor enter in and be wholly absorbed, body in body; for sometimes it seems that that is what they are craving and striving to do, so hungrily do they cling together in Venus' fetters, while their limbs are unnerved and liquefied by the intensity of rapture. At length, when the spate of lust is spent, there comes a slight intermission in the raging fever. But not for long. Soon the same frenzy returns. The fit is upon them once more. They ask themselves what it is they are craving for, but find no device that will master their malady. In aimless bewilderment they waste away, stricken by an unseen wound.

Add to this that they spend their strength and fail under the strain. Their days are passed at the mercy of another's whim. Their wealth slips from them, transmuted to Babylonian brocades. Their duties are neglected. Their reputation totters and goes into a decline. It is all very well for dainty feet to sparkle with gay slippers of Sicyon; for settings of gold to enclasp huge emeralds aglow with green fire, and sea-tinted garments to suffer the constant wear and stain of Venus. A hardwon patrimony is metamorphosed into bonnets and tiaras or, it may be, into Grecian robes, masterpieces from the looms of Elis or of Ceos. No matter how lavish the décor and the cuisine – drinking parties (with no lack of drinks), entertainments, perfumes, garlands, festoons and all – they are still to no purpose. From the very heart of the fountain of delight there rises a jet of bitterness that poisons the fragrance of the flowers. Perhaps the unforgetting mind frets itself remorsefully with the thought of life's best years squandered in sloth and debauchery. Perhaps the beloved has let fly some two-edged word, which lodges in the impassioned heart and glows there like a living flame. Perhaps he thinks she is rolling her eyes too freely and turning them upon another, or he catches in her face a hint of mockery.

And these are the evils inherent in love that prospers and fulfils its hopes. In starved and thwarted love the evils you can see plainly without even opening your eyes are past all counting. How much better to be on your guard beforehand, as I have advised, and take care that you are not enmeshed!

To avoid enticement into the snares of love is not so difficult as, once entrapped, to escape out of the toils and snap the tenacious knots of Venus. And yet, be you never so tightly entangled and embrangled, you can still free yourself from the curse unless you stand in the way of your own freedom. First, you should concentrate on all the faults of mind or body of her whom you covet and sigh for. For men often behave as though blinded by love and credit the beloved with charms to which she has no valid title. How often do we see blemished and unsightly women basking in a lover's adoration! One man scoffs at another and urges him to propitiate Venus because he is the victim of such a degrading passion; yet as like as not the poor devil is in the same unhappy plight himself, all unaware. A sallow wench is acclaimed as a nut-brown maid. A sluttish slattern is admired for her 'sweet disorder'. Her eyes are never green, but grey as Athene's. If she is stringy and woody, she is lithe as a gazelle. A stunted runt is a sprite, a sheer delight from top to toe. A clumsy giantess is 'a daughter of the gods divinely tall'. She has an impediment in her speech – a charming lisp, of course. She's as mute as a stockfish – what modesty! A waspish, fiery-tempered scold – she 'burns with a gem-like flame'. She becomes 'svelte' and 'willowy' when she is almost too skinny to live; 'delicate' when she is half-dead with coughing. Her breasts are swollen and protuberant: she is 'Ceres suckling Bacchus'. Her nose is snub – 'a Faun', then, or 'a child of the

Satyrs'. Her lips bulge: she is 'all kiss'. It would be a wearisome task to run through the whole catalogue. But suppose her face in fact is all that could be desired and the charm of Venus radiates from her whole body. Even so, there are still others. Even so, we lived without her before. Even so, in her physical nature she is no different, as we well know, from the plainest of her sex. She is driven to use foul-smelling fumigants. Her maids keep well away from her and snigger behind her back. The tearful lover, shut out from the presence, heaps the threshold with flowers and garlands, anoints the disdainful doorposts with perfume, and plants rueful kisses on the door. Often enough, were he admitted, one whiff would promptly make him cast round for some decent pretext to take his leave. His fond complaint, long-pondered and far-fetched, would fall dismally flat. He would curse himself for a fool to have endowed her with qualities above mortal imperfection.

To the daughters of Venus themselves all this is no secret. Hence they are at pains to hide all the back-stage activities of life from those whom they wish to keep fast bound in the bonds of love. But their pains are wasted, since your mind has power to drag all these mysteries into the daylight and get at the truth behind the sniggers. Then, if the lady is good-hearted and void of malice, it is up to you in your turn to accept unpleasant facts and make allowance for human imperfection.

Do not imagine that a woman is always sighing with feigned love when she clings to a man in a close embrace, body to body, and prolongs his kisses by the tension of moist lips. Often she is acting from the heart and in longing for a shared delight tempts him to run love's race to the end. So, too, with birds and beasts, both tame and wild. Cows and mares would never submit to the males, were it not that their female nature in its super-abundance is all aglow and their resistance to the generative seed is quelled by delight. Have you never noticed, again, how couples linked by mutual rapture are often tormented in their common bondage? How often dogs at a street corner, wishing to separate, tug lustily with all their might in opposite directions and yet remain united by the constraining fetters of Venus? This they would never do unless they experienced mutual joys which mock at their efforts and hold them enchained. Here then is proof upon proof for my contention that the pleasure of sex is shared.

In the intermingling of seed it may happen that the woman by a sudden effort overmasters the power of the man and takes control of it. Then children are conceived of the maternal seed and take after their mother. Correspondingly children may be conceived of the paternal seed and take after their father. The children in whom you see a two-sided likeness, combining features of both parents, are products alike of their father's body and their mother's blood. At their making the seeds that course through the limbs under the impulse of Venus were dashed together by the collusion of mutual passion in which neither party was master or mastered.

It may also happen at times that children take after their grandparents, or recall the features of great-grandparents. This is because the parents' bodies often preserve a quantity of latent seeds, grouped in many combinations, which derive from an ancestral stock handed down from generation to generation. From these Venus evokes a random assortment of characters, reproducing ancestral traits of expression, voice or hair; for these characters are determined by specific seeds no less than our faces and bodily members.

It may seem strange that female offspring is engendered from the father's seed, and the mother's body gives birth to males. The fact is that the embryo is always composed of atoms from both sources, only it derives more than half from the parent which it more closely resembles. This is noticeable in either case, whether the child's origin is predominantly male or female.

Do not imagine that fruitful seed is denied to any man by the will of the gods, so that he may never be hailed as father by winsome children but must live through a sexual life that yields no fruit. There are many who are moved by this belief to enrich the sacrificial altars with rivers of blood and the smoke of burnt offerings in the pathetic hope that their wives may be made big with unstinted seed. It is all in vain that they importune gods or fates. For the barrenness of the males is due in some cases to the over-coarse grain of the seed, in others to its excessive fineness and fluidity. The fine seed, because it cannot stick fast in its place, slips quickly away and returns abortive. The coarser type, because it is emitted in too cohesive a form, either does not travel with enough momentum, or fails to penetrate where it is required or else, having got there, fails to mix properly with the female seed. For the affairs of Venus clearly involve wide variations in harmony. Men differ in their power to impregnate different women, and women similarly in the power to receive from different men and grow big by them. Many women have proved barren in earlier unions yet have eventually found husbands by whom they could conceive little ones and be enriched with the blessings of childbirth. And men in whose homes fruitful women have previously failed to bear have at length found a complementary nature so that they too could fortify their declining years with sons.

The vital thing is to ensure the right mixture of seeds for procreation, coarse harmonizing with fine and fine with coarse. Another important factor is diet: some foods thicken the seeds in the body, others in turn thin and diminish them. A third factor of great importance is the mode in which the pleasures of intercourse are enjoyed. It is thought that women conceive more readily in the manner of four-footed beasts in a prone posture with loins uplifted so as to give access to the seed. Certainly, wives have no need of lascivious movements. A woman makes conception more difficult by offering a mock resistance and accepting Venus with a wriggling body. She diverts the furrow from the straight course of the ploughshare and makes the seed fall wide of the plot. These tricks are employed by prostitutes for their own ends, so that they may not conceive too frequently and be laid up by pregnancy and at the same time may make intercourse more attractive to men. But obviously our wives can have no use for them.

Lastly, it is by no divine intervention, no prick of

Cupid's darts, that a woman deficient in beauty sometimes becomes the object of love. Often the woman
herself, by humouring a man's fancies and keeping herself fresh and smart, makes it easy for him to share his
life with her. Over and above this, love is built up bit by
bit by mere usage. Nothing can resist the continually
repeated impact of a blow, however light, as you see
drops of water falling on one spot at long last wear
through a stone.